Copyright N

No part of this publication or creative ~~~~, distributed, or transmitted in any form ... means, including photocopying, recording, or other electronic or mechanical methods, without the prior written permission of the publisher, except in the case of brief quotations embodied in reviews and certain other non-commercial uses permitted by copyright law.

Disclaimer Notice

All subjects in the interviews, their identities and names have been excluded for their privacy and safety. No part of this book is intended to replace medical, legal, or professional mental help related to any possible topic, subject, issue or element within this book. Although the author and publisher have made every effort to ensure that the information in this book was correct at press time, the author and publisher do not assume and hereby disclaim any liability to any party for any loss, damage or disruption caused by error, omissions or analysis, whether such errors result from negligence, accident or any other cause. Any resemblance to actual persons, living or dead, or actual events is purely coincidental.

ISBN: 978-1-7334544-3-8

PUBLISHER
THE AI ORGANIZATION

4275 Executive Square, Suite 200, La Jolla, California, 92037

www.THEAIORGANIZATION.com

CO-AUTHORED:

CYRUS A. PARSA & THE SOCIAL PROGRAMMING INSTITUTE

The Social Programming Institute

The Social Programming Institute (SPI) specializes in research, decoding & consultation of Bio-Digital Social Programming as it relates to Culture, Media, Technology, AI, the Human Body, Health, Education, Families, Women, Men and Governance. www.THESPI.org

Cyrus A. Parsa, is the Founder and CEO of The AI Organization, Loyal Guardian Security and The Social Programming Institute. All created to assist in making our society safer and better. Cyrus has a Bachelor's in International Security & Conflict Resolution, and a Master's Degree in Homeland Security. He is an expert in China-Iran affairs, and has consulted on Human-Organ Tracking, Anti-Terrorism, Vulnerability, Risk, Asset Management and Emerging Threats to governments, agencies, people and organizations. He lived in the mountains of China with flighting monks as a youth. 20 years of hidden research, and development, with a network of thousands of Chinese and Westerners, allowed for great insight into the threats we face from China, Iran and the Western interconnectivity. Cyrus's discoveries have led him to coin the new concepts of "The AI Global Bio-Digital Network, The Human Bio-Digital Network, Bio-Digital Social Programming, Bio-Digital Field, Bio-Matter, Rape-Mind, Bio-Digital Hybrid Sexual Assault & Micro-Botic Terrorism" to explain how the dangers we face, and all the trouble we find ourselves in, are rooted in these almost imperceptible elements that are now connecting with AI, Society, Smart Phones, IoT, and Robotics through one platform. Within this platform, Cyrus found extinction codes.

SECTION ONE

Interviews with Bio-Digital Social Programming Consent Rape Automation Victims: Women and Men

Girl Interview with Subject 1

Girl Interview Subject 2.

Interview with Girl 3

Interviews of Men who had Sex with 50-5,000 Girls

Subject One, Man Who Slept with 5,000 Girls

Subject Two, 50 Girls from 2008-2010

Subject Three, 214 Girls from 1985-2017

Subject Four, 220 Girls from 1976-2019

Subject Five, 250-300 Girls from 1995-2019

SECTION TWO

The Beginning of Rape in History with Physical Force VS the Invisible Force of Today

Rape in History

War World II, The Socialist-Communist Regime of Russia

The Invading Mongols Raped Millions of People in the Persian, Arab and Roman Lands

Today: 20th-21st Century

Rape VIA Bio-Digital Social Programming: Invasion by Marxist/Socialist Methods to Attack Culture Rooted in Family Ethics

Early 1900's Socialist Marxist Thought led to Rape and Murder of Millions in Russia

Advertisement Promoting Rape and Sexual Revolution through Socialism in Russia 1915-1920's

1920-30's Socialism/Communist in Germany

1900-1950's Socialism in the U.S and The Rise to Sexualization of Girls

Internal Documents of the FBI

1953 Alfred Kinsey Socialist Theory of Sexualization

1953 to Now

Playboy

Penthouse

Porn

Socialist Hijacking of the Black Movement for Freedom

SECTION THREE

Bio-Digital Social Programming

How most people are Infected by a Bio-Digital Virus called Rape-Mind through the Bio-Digital Human Network?

The Human Bio-Digital Network

Rape-Mind

Bio-Digital Field

Bio-Matter

Bio-Fields & Bio-Matter Transmit Through All Avenues

How Sexual Neural Circuits are Bio-Digitally Programmed like a Virus into You to Rape or be Raped

Rape-Mind Registers in Bio-Digital Codes Measured via Your Biometrics, Coding & Human Bio-Digital Network

Facial Recognition

Brain & Vocal Cord Signal Interception Device & Software

Thought Detection Device & Software to Extract Brain Data

Infection of your Bio-Digital Field with Porn, & Lewd Content that Replicates in Your body, Brain and Mind as Rape-Mind

Facial Recognition and Porn

Emotional Programming via Bio-Digital Programming with Un-Conscious, Sub-Conscious and Conscious Rape Automation of Girls

Rape Automation

Rape Automation at Universities, Parties, Clubs and Social Encounters

Un-Conscious Rape Automation

Sub-Conscious Rape Automation

Conscious Rape Automation

IoT, Computers, and Electronic Devices

Sexual Bio-Digital Social Programming through IoT and Apps

Rap Music Registered High Frequencies & Building Blocks of Rape-Mind

10-15-Year-Old Girls Dancing to Apps that Rappers with Rape-Mind/Sexual Minds Influenced or Created

Girls Bio-Digitally Programmed with Lewd Content from Women Pop and R&B Singers that have Rape Automation Acceptance Minds in their Voice, and Gesture Outputs

Bio-Digital Sexual Programing Through Music at Your Favorite Locations

Health Club/Work Out Gyms

Prestigious Universities - Chocking, slapping, and Implying Rape Music

Coffee Shops

Censored Rape Automation in Music.

Night Clubs

Schools, Entertainment Industry and the Bio-Digital Hybrid Sexual Assault on kids.

Targeted for Bio-Digital Cultural Terrorism with Rape-Mind

Women & Men's Noble Character and Bio-Digital Attack by Rape Mind

Penetration of Our Psychologists and Therapists

Bio-Fields in Texts, Emails, Electronic Transmissions and Letters

Rapist or Malevolent Bio-Field Minds in Text, Emails, Electronic Transmissions and Letters

Rapist Bio-Field in some Psychologists, Psychiatrists and Scholars

Facial Recognition Software shows Rape-Mind of Socialist-Communist Leaders & Socialist Art Contributors Matching 1000 Serial Rapists

Rape and Destruction Bio-Field in Socialism

Bio-Fields behind the Coding of literature in Socialism/Communist Systems Derived from Karl

Marx's Communist Manifesto Shows Enslavement, Genocide and Extermination Coded Patterns.

Bio-Field of China's Communist Regime

Chinese Socialist Regimes Rape, Human, Organ and Sex Trafficking

Bio-Digital Fields in Paintings, Sculptures & Images

A Painting by Picasso Contains Bio-Digital Rape

Deep Learning of Rape-Mind Transfers to Other Painters

Picasso's Rape Mind enters Hollywood, the Education Systems, Family Homes and the Entertainment Industry through Deep Learning within the Bio-Digital Human Network

Your Smart Phone Bio-Digitally Social Programs You

Smarts Phones Bio-Field Assists in Raping a Girl through Bio-Digital Rape Automation

Apps Assists in Social Programming you, or Raping You, Your Child, or Any Girl or Boy

IoT Bio-Digital Rape Automation

IoT Bio Digital Hybrid Sexual Assault

Apps Bio Digital Hybrid Sexual Assault

Beer/Alcohol Rape Bio-Digital Social Programming

Drug Bio-Digital Social Programming with Rape-Mind

Bio-Field Proximity Rape Automation

Peer Bio-Digital Social Programming with Rape Grooming

Parent Bio-Digital Social Programming with Rape Grooming

People in Hollywood, Media and Entertainment Industry are Victims of Bio-Digital Hybrid Sexual Assault from Rape-Mind

Reminder: What is Rape-Mind

Rape-Mind and its Cultural, Faith and Governance Platforms

1. Platforms for systems of Culture, Faith and Governance

2. People

Media & Entertainment Industries Bio-Digital Social Programming of a Rape-Mind

Rape-Mind's Bio-Field Carries on Sexualized Identity Across all Human Identities like a Virus through Porn and Sexualized Lewd Content

If it's bad for kids, why isn't it bad for adults?

Sexualized Rape-Mind Consumes a Person's Identity in Dormant State

Rape Mind Bio-Digital Field Carries on One's Body

Why it is All Rape?

Instinctual Rape Programming and Societies' Non-Readiness for Commitment within Socialism

Sex Trafficked Bio-Digital Syndrome from Rape-Mind

Hybrid Bio-Digital Sexual Assault

Instruments of Bio-Digital Rape-Mind Attack - Frequencies

    Frequencies Sent Through Eyes

    Frequencies Sent Through Voice

    Frequencies Sent Through Touch

Bio-Field Frequency Proximity Rape Automation Control

Sex Tracking Software in Humans with Bio-Digital Field of Rape-Mind

False Impression Rape-Mind Automation Penetration

Platonic Friendships' External Bio-Digital Rape Decisions in Both Parties

Rape by the Red Man in Lucid Dreams Immobilizing a Girl's Body

    From Religion or Faith-based understanding

    From a Biological or Psychologists perspective

    From a technological perspective

An Alternative is an internal replicating Bio-Digital Software Sexual Assault virus

Who is to Blame for All this?

What are Repercussions?

What is the Solution?

Legal Channels, Lawsuits and the FBI

CREDITS

INTRODUCTION

This book is meant to protect women and men. I will describe how Social Programming with a rape automation component works to hurt and damage young girls, woman, men, families, and our entire society; effecting your physical health, mind, finances, and future ability to have a fulfilling life with higher opportunities. You will understand how to decode it, prevent it, counter it, and help eliminate it from your life and from society, in turn doing your part in making a better world. You will further understand a higher decoding, for which the Social Programming Institute (The SPI) has termed as Bio-Digital Social Programming, that is used in a hybrid way, penetrating your defenses in order to rape you in sub-conscious, unconscious and conscious automated ways. This rape is termed Bio-Digital Hybrid Sexual Assault, that penetrates your Bio-Digital Field and is rampant with Smart Phones, Apps, IoT devices and AI, as it utilizes a certain frequency that replicates in the human body, your nervous system, cells, and even impacts your DNA.

The bio-digital mind of a rapist bio-digitally crosses through content provided by Hollywood, Media, Music, Dance and the Education System. This mind has been termed Rape-Mind, as we have discovered bio-metric technologies that show and decode its very building blocks comprised of bio-digital fields and bio-matter. The investigator at The SPI has invested nearly 20 years of research on the Human Bio-Digital Network, and its interconnectivity with the internet, culture and governing platforms.

This book contains interviews of men that slept with 50 to 5,000 girls. Girls and women from young ages to very old were interviewed and the intelligence gathered incorporates scientific methods that include AI algorithms in conjunction with contemporary culture, media, industry, and issues related to mind-body health, growth and well-being. The book starts with interviews with victims, then takes you through a very brief history of rape and how it has transitioned to Bio-Digital Social Programming with Rape Automation that controls humanity today in imperceptible ways. Then it transitions to how new technology led by AI and Automation is actually fostering rape, sex crimes and human trafficking at a global scale outnumbering all of the war-time rapes combined. The victims are not simply girls or women, but all men as well. The concepts of Rape-Mind, Human Bio-Digital Network, Bio-Matter and Replication will be elaborated as it pertains to Rape in a multitude of ways. This is a must read for anyone interested in a meaningful relationship, and anyone who is a parent, a sister, a brother, a daughter, family, in law enforcement, in the tech industry, in education, in the media or government.

Three Sections Notice to Reader and What You Can Learn from This Precious Book

Section one will strictly include questions and answers from interviews of bio-digital social programming rape automation consent victims, that is correlated with section 2 and section 3 of the book. Section 2 will cover the history of Rape and how it developed in society in the form of Bio-Digital Social Programming with Rape-Mind in Socialist Systems. Section 3 will cover the technologies of today and how they connect to the human bio-digital network, controlling humanity. Without all sections combined one cannot truly understand the depth of this new phenomenon, how it affects you, its inter-connectedness with Smart Phones and IoT Devices working through the bio-digital human network and how the human body connects with it through bio-digital social programming.

Parts of this book may seem a bit confusing in chronology and creative content, some parts genius, and others in the realm of science fiction, especially with the incorporation of Artificial Intelligence, Facial Recognition and Human Bio-Digital Fields and Bio-Matter. I implore everyone, to read it in its entirety without emotional triggers. You can spend a lifetime in school, and never learn as much as you will in this book about Bio-Digital Social Programming and its relation to the human body and every field of study known to humankind.

SECTION ONE

Interviews with Bio-Digital Social Programming Consent Rape Automation Victims: Women and Men

Victims of Bio-Digital Hybrid Sexual Assault & Bio-Digital Social Programming

Girl Interview with Subject 1

Were you pressured into giving your virginity in your teenage years, if so, what was the situation?

Yes, 100%. All my girlfriends were dating guys and sleeping around, and they suggested and influenced me to have sex at 13 with a 17-year-old. I was in the 7th grade, he was a senior in high school.

How did you meet?

Through Facebook and we communicated with multiple online apps.

What was the process and content in your communications?

First, just sharing selfies, and making small talk in an app that everyone used. We shared a lot of pictures, and music and dance videos. We finally met at a party. I really don't know what happened. After one month of sharing videos, and dance pics, we met, there were a lot of guys and girls, everyone was drinking and he asked me to go upstairs with his friends to show me his dance moves in a quieter place. When we got up, they started to Rap about girls and some kind of dirty and nasty talk. They asked me to dance the moves that they watched me practice on the videos they made. I felt obligated, as I was dancing, they closed the door, I didn't realize it until the routine was over. There was 3 of them. They just grabbed me, one by one, and asked me to do all kinds of things I had never done before. I felt like I couldn't say no, I felt trapped in that room. All 3 ended up having sex with me within 1 hour, and taking turns with me in the room. I never said no, not once, but every ounce of me wanted to scream no, every second of it, for what it seemed like over 2 hours. I bled a lot, and they didn't care, the rap music was so loud, that nobody could hear my screams of pain. I don't know if it was because I was white, but they became really nasty to me, during. Calling me my white whore, and my white bitch, my white slave, and so on. It was really traumatic.

Did you call the police or notify the FBI?

No. I never asked them to stop, and never said no, and never pushed away, or walked away. I never voiced the words no, and never physically resisted any of their moves.

Were they all teenagers?

Yes, the one was 17, the other two were 14 and 15.

Were there any drugs involved?

No.

Did you know why you were going into that room?

As they said, to see dance moves in private as there were over 100 people in the house downstairs going out the door. My friend actually took me up there, but she walked back downstairs within 30 seconds of coming up, she was smoking a lot of Marijuana, constantly high. After that happened. One by one, they kept on calling me over to their house and their friends' houses, with pics of me dancing, before I had sex with them. I wasn't sure if they implied, they had a video, but I felt I had to go, like something was controlling me after the incident to go investigate. After the 2nd time, they started to film me. It went on like this, until I was 16 years old. I think they passed me around to more than 50 of their friends during the course of those 3 years.

Do you mean into prostitution, were you physically forced, threatened or blackmailed at any time?

No. No prostitution, and I was never threatened physically, blackmailed with videos, or physically forced. They were Just hookups at parties. They would just grab me whenever they wanted to, and share me with their friends, it even turned to girlfriends. They would imitate the porn videos, and have porn contests.

What do you mean, porn contests?

They would have a rap contest, then watch porn, and then a porn contest. Everyone would watch the girl, and rate to see if they could top the porn video.

Where were your parents?

My dad died when I was 12, and my mom would always hang with her new boyfriend, smoking Pot, and going to rock concerts. She never knew the extent of it, but she smoked Pot with her boyfriend all the time, I don't think she would have even been able to care.

You said, something controlled you, and you couldn't leave the room.

Yes. It was like a dark force in the room. The first night those 3 guys had sex with me, right before anything, I felt chills in my body, actually right after I finished that first dance and they had closed the door.

What kind of dance?

I was a cheerleader, and we had skits that played to certain songs.

What were they?

Mainly hip hop and rap.

Did you like hip hop and rap?

Not particularly, but most of the dances were created with those rhymes, and they had little quick shakes of your behind, which were not sexual as we did them in school and you see it on TV all the time.

And you did that dance right before all 3 had sex with you?

Yes, I just came from cheerleading practice.

How long were you doing these dances?

About 3 months. Before I did Ballet.

In Ballet, was there a different feeling?

Yes. In ballet, I felt like I was in control, and more focused, and it seemed, I guess more innocent.

You mean the music was different and your behind didn't make sexual moves?

Hm, thinking back, yes, ballet emphasized beauty, tranquility, grace, kindness and the music was in harmony with my calm natured self.

Were you expecting to have sex that night, with any of those guys, or to be their girlfriends?

No, not at all. He gave me a lot of compliments on my dancing, and told me he could show me a lot of new moves and that his friends were really cool and know the best ones.

Do you think it was rape in a way?

Yes, sort of, but I can't explain it. If I were to, I would say, rape with no words, and no threats, and no physical force, just control over me that made me freeze.

Was it the way they looked at you, was it threatening?

There were no threats involved, they just took action. Something right before the actions, something inside of me felt that they had broken into me before even touching me. It was weird. There was this feeling, that something invisible from them, the music, and from the room was controlling me. Thinking back, I get goosebumps. It was a cold feeling. It's really hard to describe it. You may think I am crazy saying that something controlled me, that felt cold and threatening, but it was invisible, and yet I could feel it.

Not at all. You own a smart phone and a computer I assume?

Yes.

Have you heard of the saying that the human brain is more powerful than a computer, that it just has not been tapped into?

Yea, I've heard that.

If I told you that you were raped through Bio-Digital Social Programming, and that was Bio-Digital Hybrid Sexual Assault, what would you think of these concepts? That human beings actually have a bio-field and a bio-digital system that can be attacked and manipulated?

Well, the idea that I was social programmed, resonates, not sure what you mean about bio, but you are saying by some kind of technology they used on me?

Not exactly. I am saying something entirely different. But you get the social programming, right?

Yes, they set me up, and were nice to me and tricked me to get into that room, and he was nice to me for one whole month via the APP, and super nice in person.

That's part of it. But you said, you felt an invisible, cold substance or energy, is that correct to describe it in that way?

Yes, like a force.

What did you watch before you met them, before the "Force penetrated you and you felt helpless and froze" what was the type of music, content and was it on your smart phone?

We had cheerleading practice, then they sent me a bunch of rap music videos. The videos had rappers with blonde girls all around them, and some other video's showed girls shaking their hips in a contest.

You are blonde, correct? And your smart phone, did you practice those dances yourself?

Yes, on both. It was something everyone was doing on social media; You Tube and Facebook.

So, it felt natural by the time you got to meet them at the house?

Yes, totally.

Did you feel a need to look at your phone a lot, especially at those video's they sent you prior to getting to their house, if so, was it for practice, for interest, or you're mind gave you the idea to look at your phone and those videos?

Not a lot, but I looked at them repeatedly. I would say, the thoughts just popped into my head to look, even before my friend drove us there.

Thinking back, those videos by the rappers, the ones you download from the music industry, are there subliminal messages that treat girls like sex slaves or a piece of meat they can own?

Before, I'd say no, now, looking back, now I say, yes, the lyrics are even nasty. I never bothered to mention them before.

You mentioned your mom went to rock concerts a lot. What is the feeling rock gives you?

That you are free, sort of free to do anything, I guess, its mostly joyful. My mom was actually in a rock band. She ended up leaving my dad for some guy in a band she played with, right before he died. And since then, she has gone from one dude to another. Growing up, I could hear my dad always complaining that she cared more about partying than the family.

Getting back to the "Invisible Force" and the cold feeling touching your body. Think back, since you seem to be a little sensitive more so than most people. Did you feel this invisible force, and the cold reach something around you, that was part of you, but was not your skin, sort of something that belongs to you, that is you, but is sort of around you, may be an inch to 2 inches before the perimeter of your body, before it hits your hairs and skin?

Ah, come to think of it, yes, well, yes, I felt it touch me, before it reached me, not a human touch, or a hand, but something that reached me. Like it touched something around me, then I got scared, than I felt it on my skin, and then I froze, as I felt it inside me, and right after, they physically grabbed, hugged me, and asked me to dance in a certain way, while they were holding me. And then from there, I had lost all control, they kept on touching me, and dancing, and asked me to do a lot of dirty things I had never done before. What was strange was, I had never done them before, but something led me to know how to do them, and do them exactly the way they wanted it. It was a combination of them telling me, leading me a long, and something moving me to do things I had never done before.

You know, a computer can be programmed to do things by software, that is not even seen with the naked eye. What I am

trying to share with you is, that there is actually a bio-digital field around people, and it can connect with others, through touch, voice, sight, being in proximity, through thought, and more importantly, strengthened exponentially through IoT devices, Smart Phones and even Apps. The same things Robots and devices can do, humans can actually do, they just don't know how. But people are a part of it, and almost completely controlled bio-digitally by a Rape-Mind and degrading culture that was heavily implemented into the U.S. in the 1950's and became full blown in the 1960's. What is your perception of the 1940s and 50s, since you were not yet born then?

It's strange, any image I've seen in movies of the 1950's, people seemed classy, and really family oriented and I don't think they slept around, right?

They usually got married after high school, men worked, women worked to raise the kids, together they were a team and the family unit strictly watched over the kids, and the culture and upbringing didn't come from the few people from the entertainment industry and Hollywood. No, people didn't sleep around like today, and Sexual Transmitted diseases were not rampant like today, with all the health problems and medication, and certainly, there was a lot less rape. Platonic friendships hardly existed the way they do now. I thank you for your sharing.

Girl Interview Subject 2

How did you lose your virginity?

It was great at first, and I think it put a scar in me for life, after. I trusted him, he told me he loved me, 2 months of courtship went by, after he took my virginity and moved to another girl, I fell into despair, couldn't eat, and could never trust another man.

He implied he would marry you or stay with you and if so, did he plan to just get your virginity?

Yes, that was the case, I didn't realize it until the day after, as his compliments, and way of being completely changed. I found out, he was dating 2 other girls at the same time, and he was into porn and nude magazines.

What kind of music did he and you listen to?

I listened to classical music and played the violin; he was into rap and hip hop and hard rock.

What happened to you after that?

I was in depression for 6 months, I had a wish to marry one guy, grow together, have kids, travel, see our kids grow, and have a good life. I started making friends with men with no intent of having sex and made that known. After hanging out with the boys, I ended up having sex with everyone one of them. I felt like trash, and used, but during the time, was under the influence of drugs and drinking beer and lots of wine. In fact, my taste in music changed, I stopped playing the violin, and would dance in dirty ways to Rap and Hip Hop. I felt like a sex slave, but couldn't get out of it. It was a strange situation. They knew I didn't want to, but through different ways, they got me to do different things, and then I felt like I couldn't do anything, in their presence, I felt I had no control over my mind, or will, and was, used for sex. I never said no, but I felt, like there was a force inside them, that controlled me, it was like rape, but I never said no, couldn't' say no, and I never physically pushed any of them away. But, something inside me, that actual me, couldn't move, as every ounce of me wanted to scream no, and not be in their presence, but felt controlled.

Do you think it's possible that a human body has a bio-digital program, connected by digital/electrical circuits that are connected to your brain and values, and that system can be attacked, influenced and corrupted by others Bio-Fields, Voice, Touch and Visual Senses? It's that system that actually can get raped, or penetrated, once it is penetrated, there is a disconnect and weakened connection with your actual body, and other peoples Bio-Digital information and operations can take over your body?

I don't exactly know what all that means in terms of the language you just used, but it feels a lot like what happened to me. Like there was an invisible force when I was around these boys, and the environment I was in with the music, and drugs, that completely controlled my body and brain, and desensitized my true-self.

Did you come from a religious background?

My parents were catholic in name, but my dad cheated on my mom and vice versa. My father was addicted to playboy magazines and the porn he had stashed away. And my mother always made excuses to meet her male cohorts for lunch, but I knew what she was doing. She was addicted to watching VH1, MTV and Soap Operas instead of spending quality time with my dad. I don't know if that played any part in influencing her. I don't even know if my dad did it first, or it was my mother. I know they both cheated on each other, and both contracted STD's according to my mom. They were virgins when they were married, with no sexual diseases. Seeing that, I knew I shouldn't fall into that world like them. I was mostly impacted by the cartoon Cinderella, and wanted to be a good person and marry a good man, and be loyal to each other.

To answer your question, I was not religious, just optimistic for a good life with a good man.

Do you think it's possible all of America was actually programmed to break the traditional and family unit, to hurt the U.S through Media, Music, TV, Movies, and the Education System? And that program was cleverly installed and promoted by Russian Marxists/ Socialists before the 1950s? That that boy who hurt you and changed the course of your life, was programmed to do so? That all the guys who fed you drugs, alcohol and had sex with you, were programmed to do so? And you were programmed to be in that situation as were many other girls? That the entire society got penetrated with a bad code that hurts people? That what happened to you was a form of rape, but in steps through a Bio-Digital Social Program?

I don't know much about socialism, I do know it came from Marxism, and lots of people died and went hungry because of it. But seeing scenes of the 1940's and 1950's, there was a beauty about it, with the family unit and the courtship. All of that was turned upside down. And it seems one thing led to another. The rape part, yes 100%... Absolutely 100%. I felt my body and mind were raped before I was actually physically raped. I never called it rape, but felt it was. But it felt like something was destroyed in me first, then I gave into the sex. Any raping actually happened before the actual sex. The rest was just a continuous cycle that I was in, and I couldn't' get out of it for months or years from one guy onto another after these groups of guys were done with me. It was as if they trained me, before I ever did anything, and continued to train me, and I lived that way, until I was an emotional mess, addicted to medication, drinks, and Marijuana. There was something in me, that actually got addicted to having one-night stands, that made me live that way, and I couldn't stop, until I got sick and developed Sexually Transmitted Diseases.

Did you feel like you were in an automated mode from the imprinting and mindsets you received from those guys?

Hm, thinking back, yes, it totally felt that way.

Do you think it's possible that if a computer has a software and hardware, your software can be corrupted and reprogrammed with other people's programs through not only the training they gave you, but the physical contact you made with them repeatedly? Meaning, your system was trained to follow that path in a way that you couldn't get out of it?

Wow, that totally makes sense. I always wanted out, but it was as if my will couldn't come through, as if I was controlled. Wow, that is a really smart way to describe it.

I mean more than that. That like a computer, your body and brain actually got imprints from these guys and the environment you were in, similar to virus's and malware that computers get. That actually your Bio-Digital field or Bio-Sphere was invaded, corrupted, and put in reprogram mode with those men's Bio-Digital fields that made up their thoughts, and way of being?

That is really, really, deep, and somehow, that makes total sense. I can't explain it, but that explanation, in my gut feeling, I totally understand it and it feels totally like what I went through. Like I was trapped.

Well, I administered a study of nearly 100,000 people with something like an AI system, using facial recognition and biometrics, all the results point to the conclusion, that what people see, hear and touch, actually have a Bio-Digital code and property, that goes into their bodies and brain, and to

varying degrees reprograms them, without their awareness. Moreover, the study concluded, that people's characters and what is in their minds, actually exists like a code in the lyrics they sing, even the movements they make, and digital products such as the movies they make. A gangster rapper, or pop star who is on drugs, a sex addict, and comes from a broken home, actually has all those imprints stored in them digitally, and too often, their negative factors are Bio-Digitally re-programming the masses who take in their entertainment, their music in a very bad way, that gives birth to rape automation. If you think about it, all of that, goes in peoples pre-existing digital software, lays dormant, manipulates them, and reprograms them to varying degrees. For example, lots of boys watch porn that is similar to rape, and the code of the people who make it and display that code in visual video formats, is pretty sick, demented, and looks at woman as sex slaves to abuse. Those imprints get programmed to young boys, men, and even women to accept being used in that way, and they pass it on like a parasitical epidemic in society, hurting families and everything connected with people.

That all sounds like science fiction in one way, but in another way, I can only say, it totally makes sense with my experiences. Totally makes sense of society. Wow. If I thought of things in that way, and had this awareness, I would never have made the mistakes I have, and would not be where I am today.

Interview with Girl 3

How did you lose your virginity?

I didn't want to actually, not at all. I wanted to get married with someone I loved. My mother left my dad, and she and her parents, my grandparents, were very liberal. They smoked Marijuana, and played rock and roll all the time, were hippies and always preached that I should live, be free and have as much fun as possible, date, be happy. And they really hated the concept of morality and faith. I had no idea, either way. My mom had a new boyfriend it seemed like every week. That influence, and them actually teasing me of being uptight, got me to change at 15. By the time I was 20, I had gone through 10 boyfriends, and may be 5 hook ups, I ended up getting STD's and addicted to Marijuana and beer.

What happened to your dad? Was he religious?

Actually, he was, but I never got to be around him after 14. My mom divorced him, and got the judge to say he was aggressive in his faith, and got some kind of agency to monitor him, and argue that he was oppressive to girls who wanted freedom to choose, and that he was aggressive towards the family, calling them names like "immoral liberals that hurt the world, families and women" and wouldn't let me have friends. I witnessed him actually shout that to my mom, and telling her that her faith was sealed with immorality, and that she was harming me. At the time, I thought maybe my dad was crazy.

What kind of friends, why wouldn't he let you have friends?

Ah, guy friends. He was strictly against a girl having male friends, or me having girlfriends from families he called immoral, drug users and hateful intolerant people towards faiths or traditional family values, and what he called "America's true culture of family, and decency".

So, would you say, your idea of being with one guy, came from him or his religion, a movie you saw, something you heard?

No, not at all. Since I was 10, I wished to have one guy, and my dad was always at work, I never actually saw him, other than dinner once a week, and I never even had a faith, I just felt that that's the smart and good thing to do, and the thought of being with so many people, even more than one person, was dirty.

What happened?

My mom encouraged me to date, and I did. He pressured me into having sex, and broke if off within one week. I cried for almost 1 month, every night, going to bed. My mom told me it was natural, and that I need to just experiment so I know who to pick, and have fun. So, I dated another guy, he said he loved me, after 3 months, I agreed to have sex with him, and he ended up cheating on me. The first guy was white, this guy was half Asian and half black, and not white like the first one. I thought he'd be different, maybe wouldn't have the American way, but I was judging solely on race, as the same thing happened with an Arab guy as well, he had sex with me, and left within 5 minutes, but before that, he was so nice. He was really addicted to porn, and my mom would dress me up before our dates in high heels, mini-skirts, with tight fitting shirts, all framing my hips, chest, and made sure, as she called it, I looked "sexy". Her favorite show was "Sex and the City", we'd watch it together with her boyfriend's. After him, I didn't date anyone for 2 years. I started college, I met this charming guy, I don't know how he got me to, but after hanging out the first time, he got me to have sex, and the next day I saw him walking with another girl. I felt used, and hated the concept of love and marriage, and started dating any guy that hit on me, and started to have a lot of sex, even with girls. It seemed like, I got old really fast, and my skin got really bad in college. I started drinking, and what stopped it for me, was STD's, even though they all wore condoms, I got Std's. From the age of 15-20, it was as if I had something on me head, and it was not me, like I was not in control of myself. Today, I have had sex with round 30 guys, and did sexual things with another 20, may be. That was a lot, but it seemed everyone was doing this. Almost all friends had some sort of STD and later, got on medication for depression.

What happened to your dad?

He died of a heart attack when I was 17.

And your mom?

She dated like over 100 guys, now she is alone, smokes weed after she gets home from work, drinks, and goes to bed, and occasionally she attends Rock Concerts that come to our city. That is her life today.

And you, how is your dating life, or marriage?

I got in a long-term relationship, but it never worked out, we both had too much emotional baggage from our past relationships. I was on medication, and he was addicted to weed, porn and always wanted to date other girls. He'd always claim outlandish things, like, Ah, in Mexico, we date around, so we can do that in our relationship. He ended up being arrested in Mexico for rape of a 12-year-old, from what I heard, and assisting in sex tracking of some American girls, when he was visiting his family. After him, I haven't dated anyone in over 1 year.

How did you manage to get in a relationship with him?

I don't know, he lied really well. He sold me the Mexican culture, and always bragged that he was part Arab, part Mexican, and Part White, and Part Black and that he was different from all the other guys I was with and that I was different from the Mexican girls he was with. I had been with all kinds of guys, first guys were white, then black, Asian, Arab, and Mexican, so his boosting about some kind of culture, didn't make sense to me.

Are you partially Mexican descent and why do you bring up peoples race in the descriptions?

No, some kind of European mutt. I assume English, German, and I think I have some French, and may be a little bit from Greek and Turkish. The race thing, I don't know, I thought maybe someone would have a good culture with values, in my mind I tried every type of person, even probably made-out with another 20 guys in addition to the people I had sex with. Everyone, seems nowadays to be the same. And the more I did, it felt like I was getting worse, heavier, but something inside me wanted more.

This last guy you mentioned, He lied to get you?

More than that. He sort of made moves, got me drunk, and got me to have sex with him.

What do you mean by moves?

I can't explain it, just that he was super clever, and knew how to play me. It was as if, he at the right time, and right place, made the exact amount of eye contact, touch, and said what I needed to hear, to earn my trust, and pressured me in weird ways to have sex with him with a promise to commit.

Weird Ways?

It's hard to explain. It was like, he had a spell on me, if you'd believe that. Like mind control or something. And he knew, right off the bat, that I'd been with like 20-30 guys. He even said it. And he bragged that he'd been with over 100 girls, mostly white, and that I was the most special one.

Let me ask you. Do you feel like you were at some point conditioned, or programmed, through external forces, to make these bad decisions?

Now that I think of it, yea, like I said, there was like this junk in my head, and it was leading me on a path to destruction. What stopped me, at least for now, was the combination of the STD's, feeling and looking much older, needing so much makeup. Like, I look back, I had this beautiful glow and red cheeks on my face before all the sex, you could see in my pictures, and it's all gone, and I look like 15 years older than the one friend I had, who married at 18 some guy, who was actually a lot older, and she has 3 kids, and he was the only guy she was with. I'd imagine having 3 kids, would wear you out. But she was like a moralist, little weird, never drank, never did drugs, and never slept around, never even kissed anyone until her husband. The weird thing was, she didn't even have a religion, and both her parents were radical people, whom she told me she always hated their values and mindsets. And now she is totally content and happy. Thinking back, the judge, society, my mother, rock and roll, rap, the movies, everything and everyone portrayed or said my father who is now dead from the heart attack, was a stupid man, and ancient, and he was wrong. Now, I wish, someone guided me not down the path that I went. Society is so messed up.

Do you have a religion?

No. I don't know even if I believe in a God.

Then, why have these values now?

It just makes sense, and looking back, although I am not religious, all faiths have an understanding about sex before marriage, and it really makes sense to me. To marry someone, and both committed for life, and be ready for each other.

Getting back to "weird ways and the spell on you". Did he watch porn, do drugs, what kind friends did he have, and can you describe more clearly, if there was a physical sensation of

how you were physically controlled to make decisions you did not want to make?

I don't know, I'd call it magic, in a joking way. Is that what you are asking?

Do you think, that what you see, hear and touch, can program you, and program others in an automated way, so the decisions they make are not really theirs at all, but those implanted programs that run their course against peoples true consciousness innately in them, which tells them, what is right and wrong?

Yes, 100%, after my experience, 100%. Don't even think he was sincere in staying with me, just like the first few guys and the guy who took my virginity. They lied to me in different ways.

Well, do you think raping someone physically vs programming them with strategic emotional moves via speech, touch, and sight, is a clever form of rape?

Totally, that's exactly what happened to me.

Do you think your mom and grandparents were programmed to subconsciously program you, and vehemently attack traditional culture and contribute to where you are today?

Hm, I'd think that was their own beliefs and yes, they prevented my father from protecting me, and my brother got into porn and the night club scene and didn't care.

Ok. You have come to 2 points here. That you were influenced, programmed and tricked to have sex with those who didn't want to stay with you. That it is a form of clever rape, and your mom influenced that somehow. And that drugs and music she listened to, the performers and songs that had those values, and your boyfriends who watched porn, and did drugs, and society blasting those things all over products, tv, music, dance, and movies, and even the education system, harmed you. My question is, if the 1940's was not like that, and the women's movement was about equal rights, equal pay, the right to vote, and not be used as sex slaves in media, print and the entertainment industry, what do you think caused it?

I don't know. The media? The movies that constantly show sex, and dating one after another?

Some people in the media may just be a tool, there was probably not a conspiracy, other than some individual's hatred towards traditional values. What actually started everything was Communist/Marxist/Socialist ideologies that were implanted strategically in the U.S, to destroy the family unit and the strength of the country. You can research that if you like. You kind of described it in your experiences to a degree. What do you think of the terms Bio-Digital Hybrid Sexual Assault that can happen during Bio-Digital Social Programming?

Hm, Very neat words. Totally interesting. I think I totally get the Social Programming part, the Bio-Digital, not sure, but I feel what you're saying.

The concept is, that if a computer can get virus's, malware, and even be controlled and reprogrammed with IoT devices, uploads, and downloads through voice, touch and visual commands, so can human beings by other human being's physical presence and the content they create through music, dance, speech and writing.

Their visual and audio content literally reprograms your cells, organs, and Bio-Digital and Bio-Field to varying degrees, creating an automated system rewriting your own free-willed decisions that align with concepts of virtue that give society a

healthy mind and body. That programming itself, can actually control your decisions through connecting with your bio-digital field, and control your decisions and allow others to rape you in clever ways. Do you understand this concept or is it too hard to believe?

I think a lot of technology is coming out, before everyone thought they were science fiction. But, you are trying to say something really different I think, like there is technology in the people, that we don't see and computers and technology somehow affect people too. Coming down to this part of the interview, I'd say my grandparents, my mother and may be society would think it's a little crazy, but genius, and my dad, who was right, but could never explain it like you just did, would totally agree with you. I will, I think, I agree with that wholeheartedly. I agree with your, I'd say, genius assessment of the world.

I'd be stupid not to agree with it, after having the experiences I did. If I knew what I know now, I would have never done the things I did. My father's life was ruined, mine is in ruins, my mother is in ruins, our family never had a chance.

I am sorry, we should end the interview here. I thank you for sharing. It is the wish of The Social Programing Institute, to get society to help understand this concept of Bio-Digital Social Programming, since my goal here, is not merely about rape, and hurt families, as there are bigger things at stake now. But this is a start.

Thank you for letting me understand, I can know how not to be manipulated again. And if I have a child, I will know how to raise it well.

Interviews of Men who had Sex with 50-5,000 Girls

Subject One, Man Who Slept with 5,000 Girls

How did you manage to sleep with 5,000 girls?

Boy, it was the late 60's, 70's and 80's, sex was blasted everywhere. It was you know, my speech, smile and sharp deep eye contact and the way I moved. It helped that I had a sports car, sexual appealing furniture in a very nice house, money, good cooking and booze. I just got good at it, it was very easy, the girls were very easy, one touch and my good looks added to the mix, and boom.

Where did you meet the girls?

Schools, bars, malls, through friends, and the street. Anywhere I could make a conversation. A Hi, and compliment, a smile with penetrating eye contact, or offer to help someone with a hand in doing anything.

Do you regret the 5,000 number, meaning would you replace it with only 1 woman you loved and was happy with?

It was a hit and run time, I, looking back, during the times, I was in a zone, the more I did, the more I wanted it, and the more I needed it, and it was moments of fun, many moments, but yet, I would trade it all for one girl I loved and was happy with. I suffered a lot in this life, and I think its related to having sex with those girls. But yea, Bam, I was in and out before they knew what happened. It was the times and the locations, the music and the movies and environment made everything easier. It was hit and run. Ahhh, the universe did make me suffer for all of it, I suffer still today.

Do you feel mixed about it, you seem in one hand thrilled at doing it when recollecting, and today in remorse?

Well, I was, I was young, and stupid and just wanted to enjoy everything. Now looking back, it was not much enjoyment, kind of nasty, and it stays with me as a man and I suffer for it, a lot.

Do you think what you did can be taken as rape? Don't you think you made them love you, stole their virginity, broke their hearts and ran off to the next one?

Well, for the non-virgins, most of them wanted it, so in that case, it was natural for me, but some virgins, yes, I really hurt them. And I suffered for all of them.

What about the non-virgins, you made them like you, and got them into doing sexual things with your social techniques, isn't that not right, didn't you hurt them?

It's the way it is. They wanted it. The world is that way, you're not going to change it overnight. Look at Hollywood, look at America, everyone is doing it. It's a place of sluts, and drugs, and fakes, there is no family anymore like the 1940s and 1950's. Women used to be classy, beautiful from the inside out in their character, men would respect them with Ms. or Mrs. Even if you're not a slut, society makes you behave like one, you fall inside that garbage and lose your humanity. Before you had the family and feelings of decency.

Your calling some or a lot of women and men names, by your own definition, what does that make you?

Well, just the same. What do you think it makes us?

In my view, everyone is a victim of a system that was created and influenced by a very small percentage of people from a system to hurt not only girls, but humanity. For you, if the number of 5,000 is true, you are in a different field, and I thank you for sharing your methods and stories.

About the 5,000 girl's number, that is hard to imagine, how do you come up with it?

Well, for 10 years straight, it was 1 a day, sometimes 2 new ones in a single day. You count the late 60's, the 70 the 80s and early 90's, 3-4 decades worth. In some decades it was may be 2-3 a week. I think, that was the 90's when I was slowing down. Boy, if I was young in today's time, with the way things are, I think the number would be much higher. I got to that number by counting mostly the U.S, may be a few hundred in Europe during my travels, and 50 or so in the Middle East behind the scenes when their family wasn't looking. America's culture was alive behind the scenes there too, through movies and music.

Last question, would you really change the 5,000 girls for 1 you love today? Take back all those behaviors that a lot of men would consider pleasure, for only 1 person you would have to be faithful with your entire life? Of Course, in this scenario she would be respectful and faithful to you and a good match?

Yes, 100%. Those girls were trained by societies influences to accept what I was trying to do, and I was on a rampage. Looking back, it was all bad, and it's worse today. I really wish I was with just one girl and we lived a good and decent life together. Looking back, that is my wish now.

I guess one more topic question would be fitting. Honestly, if you had a daughter, and someone tried to manipulate your daughter

to be used for sex and succeed and she ended up crying home, what would you do?

It wouldn't happen, I'd be watching her and protecting her.

Well let's say someone with half your social skills came in, but wasn't actually a friendly person, and was nasty to her, used her, and broke her heart and treated her like garbage?

I'd, ahh, I'd kill him.

Literally, you'd kill them?

No, but I'd want to, I just wouldn't let that happen, I would be a responsible parent.

But you're not even a parent.

Yes, I don't have that honor, I messed up big time.

5,000 girls and no kids?

Yes, I always used contraceptives.

How do you know you don't have a lot of your kids around the world?

I don't. I often think that I may, but didn't keep track of any of the girls. It was hit and run.

Are you sure your conduct can't be considered rape?

Well, may be in ancient times, if society wasn't the way it was today, then It would be considered rape. Kind of like a fox that makes friends with baby sheep, and devours her later.

Did you ever consider it rape before?

No, I was just in the zone.

Could you consider it rape today, from a higher, kinder, truthful and caring perspective, a sense of respect and decency for your fellow human being?

Yes, I guess you could say that, looking at it that way, the entire society is involved in promoting the rape culture without calling it rape.

What do you think it's called?

Freedom.

Is it really freedom, or do you think there are components that have actually made people programmed to be raped without realizing their decisions were not their own?

Yes, that's a very interesting way of looking at it. People's minds are programmed to be raped, ha, that is so interesting, in a way, yes.

Do you think they are programmed to be raped by people, media, education or society?

All of it. Wow, thinking back, yes, all of it. That zone I was in, it's like a program that you just mentioned. I was programmed to get these girls and they were programmed to let me in there. Like, I was programming them and society gave me the tools and prepared them for me. It be like a wolf being led into a pen of dumb innocent sheep that were kept there by a farm purposely to feed the wolves in town.

How would you solve this issue, you being one of the biggest benefactors, with 5,000 girls?

The dam media, music and movies, they promote it and make your body and mind just follow it.

Did you every use drugs to get these girls in a state to want to have sex with you?

May be 1% of them, the majority was good old drinking, food, and my communication skills. I mean, I had a system, it worked 9 out of 10 times. If it wasn't' the food, it was the smile, eye contact, touch, places we went, the ambiance, and most importantly, my energy. I had a lot of energy.

What you mean by energy?

From childhood, I had this energy, when it came to women, all I had to do was use it.

Use it like how?

I don't know, it just came and I used it with eye contact, touch, smile and my words.

Is this an energy you could see?

No, something I could feel. The more I did it, the more sex I got, the more it grew.

So, you used this energy to get girls to sleep with you, but you didn't intend to stay with them?

Some I wanted to stay with, yes, but most no.

Energy, did you do some kind of meditation or join a physics research institute? What do you mean by energy?

I can't explain it. I just had this energy that came in me and I used it.

Are you a religious person?

No, not at all.

Do you study science?

No.

Then would you say, invisible energy exists and how do you know it is real?

Yes, and it's a gut feeling, and a real feeling that I have had 40 years of experience with getting girls to sleep with me.

If frequencies that are invisible to the naked eye can be connected through devices, and program actions of cell phones, computers and even robots, would you say it is similar to people connecting with people and programming them, could there be a frequency people can send out through their eyes, voice, touch and thought?

Wow, I never thought of it that way, really strange question and interesting way of analyzing and explaining how it works.

But your experience with 5,000 girls leads you to say you used some kind of energy with your words, eye contact, touch and settings that you were in?

Yes, that is a great explanation. Yes, that is it. I can't explain it, but I guess it worked like a computer and the internet.

Do you feel like you still have that energy today?

No, if feels mostly gone actually, gone with my youth. And I suffer for it.

Could that energy or let's say focus been used to build more positive things, and a good marriage with one person for your entire lifetime?

That's long gone, I made so many mistakes, I truly regret it, truly regret them all. I guess you are right, I fail victim to a program my whole life.

Subject Two, 50 Girls from 2008-2010

In 2 years, you were with 50 girls, was there a component of seeing them as sex tools?

Not sure, I just felt the need.

What led to that?

I don't know. May be, it was a need to prove something to myself, and get as much as I wanted from them sexually.

How and where did you get to meet them and so easily have sexual relations with them?

Social media and mainly business connections with friends and associates.

Was there a component of manipulation?

No.

What about manipulation through the way you represented your character?

I suppose, yes. I gave the impression that I was always nice, had a nice job and rich family. That made it a lot easier.

At what point did you move on to the next one?

When they got attached to me and wanted a relationship.

So, did you give them that impression prior, impression of commitment?

I gave them no impression, maybe that's what girls want deep down.

Did you know that could happen prior to engaging in sexual relations with them?

No.

What about at a subconscious level, meaning you took steps to get to sleeping with them through impressions and what you said and how you said it at different times, and knowing full well at what point she would put down her guard?

May be at a subconscious level, yes, I was aware and those thoughts would come in my head, but I would never voice them.

So, you hid your thoughts?

Yes.

If you were honest in your motives, do you think the number would have been 50?

May be 25, but the girls were open to it. They had already gone through that process.

You mean desensitized?

You could say that.

What do you think led to this desensitization?

Hm. The experiences they had.

What do you think shaped the experiences they had?

The men they encountered and the friends they had.

What do you think shaped the men they encountered and friends they had?

Hm, well, the world.

What was the world like before that shaping?

I suppose everyone grew up, married their first love, had careers, and grew old together.

What and why do you think that changed?

I don't know.

How and who do you think made that change in the mainstream?

Hm, probably mainstream media, movies and the music industry. Madonna, Michael Jackson, and the rappers were big in my life and they made me think of things differently. However, movies played a big role.

Would you agree, the entertainment industry changed or gave the values we have today or greatly influenced it?

I would say so. I often saw movies of divorce and unhappiness in movies and happy people having sex with strangers and friends.

Then do you think that led your perceptions on commitment?

Yes, and no. I was really addicted to porn and playboy magazines. It made me want to have sex with as many girls as possible. And I treated the women like dirt, with disconnecting right after. Like, they were like nothing to me, in fact, but I was always nice to them on the surface.

Nice until you left them?

Well, I made sure they didn't have a bad impression, just told them rationally that I'm not feeling it anymore.

But you knew prior to being with them that you weren't feeling it anymore, would you not agree?

Hm, okay, yes.

Isn't that hiding your feelings, and true intentions?

Hm, in a way. What is your point here?

My point is, you hurt them because you hid your true intentions, that itself is manipulation, and deception in order for them to agree emotionally, or in an automated fashion to go along with whatever you wanted them to do with you. Would you agree with that?

Yes, but they knew what they were doing?

What do you mean?

Well, they came to my house, at night alone, what do they expect.

Were any of them virgins and expecting long term relationships?

May be 3-4, and yea, they really took it very, very hard. So, in their case, I totally see what you are getting at, and in retrospect, I may have hurt them through my selfish desires, not considering the aftermath.

Would you say your selfish desires were controlled or heavily influenced by the porn, playboy magazines, music and movies you viewed?

I think they strengthened them greatly. Yes, I can see that. They made me be ultra-aggressive in my view towards women. I saw them as sex objects and it was as if I was on automatic mode. And the way girls dressed fed into the feeling that they were just for sex.

What's the difference between physically raping someone vs manipulating their mind and emotions to make decisions to have sex with you based on false pretenses or implications of commitment?

I see what you are getting at. Well, the outcome is the same, one way of course is very traumatic physically and mentally. The one you are accusing me of, may be breaks their heart, and rapes their mind a bit and leaves lasting deep emotional impressions.

Did you feel a difference between the virgin's vs non virgin's emotional states?

Yes, the experienced girls, saw it as an act, the virgins saw it as something special and sacred.

What would you think of the idea that you were bio-digitally social programmed to do what you did with these girls? Meaning the magazines, movies, videos and music you took in, actually took in the software programming of those musicians, writers and movie stars state of mind, character, belief and desires? In turn, it controlled your negative side or enhanced your sexual desires in a negative way, in automatic drive? You did use the word automatic mode; one subject used the word the zone and another said "sex was in the air".

Hm. I do cyber work and I have years of coding experience. That concept actually makes sense. That is an incredible way to look at it. Hm. I do know I regret it a lot. So, you are saying, the actual character of the person, their thoughts, and desires has a code, and gets downloaded to you and either reprograms you, or corrupts your system?

Yes, that is part of what I am saying. I am also saying, that Bio-Digital Social Program actually has raped hundreds of millions of girls, and ruined millions of men, and millions of

more families and contributed to billions of interconnected issues, and the music, movie, and media industry has taken the lead in hurting humanity. In fact, it retrains your cells, and your entire brain as the code replicates itself in the body.

So, you are saying, I was programmed, and so were the girls?

To varying degrees, yes. What do you think is the biggest Bio-Digital Social Programming factor?

Hm, in my view, probably social media.

What would you think of the idea that ideas derived from Karl Marx, Communism and Socialism led to the breaking down of families and the rape and ruining of so many girls' lives?

I studied Marxism in school. The teachers all presented it in a cool way. But my parents escaped Socialism and told me of the atrocities and murders of their nation. So, I researched for myself, studied how tens of millions were murdered with socialist ideas in China, Russia, North Korea, Vietnam and Cambodia, I wouldn't put it past them. Everywhere they offered free stuff and equality, but made entire societies slaves of the socialist movements, turned families against each other and completely broke up the family structure. The term Bio-Digital Social Programming is actually a very interesting term, how did you come up with it?

People are programmed emotionally, and that emotion is social, and has frequencies that it connects through the senses, whether to send out something or receive something. And the substance it connects with and downloads can change its biochemistry. Bio-Digital Social Programming is a concept that is similar to mind-body, but it's an attempt in a sophisticated way to explain how technology in conjunction with human contact affects our world.

Thank you.

Subject Three, 214 Girls from 1985-2017

How did you sleep with 214 girls and what methods did you use?

Mainly my money and gifts attracted them as friends, and drugs and booze finished the job.

Did any of them expect sex?

May be half, the other I attracted as friends through my business.

You stated drugs and booze, did they expect drugs and booze?

About half were there for drinking and drugs, the other half I had them try it.

You mean drugs?

Yes, drugs, and alcohol, after the drugs and alcohol, then they did anything I wanted.

If the component of drugs and alcohol were not at your parties, I assume they were parties or gatherings. If they did not exist there, do you think you would have slept with 214 girls?

No, only the ones that I made feel I loved them or the ones that really wanted some favor or money. Still alcohol and drugs were a component that was needed sometimes. Probably about a quarter, may be about 50 girls would be the number today.

Is there an art to getting the girls to sleep with you?

Well, society was changing, the girls were free to spend more time away from their families, unsupervised and the party scene was everywhere.

What era was it that the party scene was not everywhere?

In the 40's and 50's, and it got really bad in the 80's with cocaine and weed.

What instigated this party scene?

I'd say the movies we watched, the books we read, playboy magazine and the music we listened to and the media.

What percentage of people you think controlled the movies and music industry?

Interesting question, probably very, very, few people with the same mindset.

You mentioned you made them feel like you loved them, was it a lie, or did you really feel like you loved them when you were trying to get them to have sex?

Ahh, I loved a handful, at least I thought I did, after having sex, I realized the love was just an emotion controlling me to tell them what they wanted to hear so that I can get in their pants.

And the Others?

I made them feel important and that I liked them a lot and interested in what they were about and doing.

You mentioned playboy, what impact did that have on you and society?

It made me think of girls more so as sex objects that I can control and own, rather than human beings. I acted suave and wanted a bachelor life instead of creating a family with someone I loved. A lot of girls and families were hurt you could say.

Then, what about porn?

I would say that trashed the beauty and mystery of love, sex, marriage and family life.

Trashed for you, or for the girls?

I think for all people and society. In my time, the people who had a desire to look at other people naked or having sex were perverts, creeps they called them. People who were mentally sick, conniving, cheated on their wives or husbands, and could not be loyal. Basically, they couldn't cut it and be responsible to their families, they couldn't respect females beyond sexualizing them.

Were you addicted to playboy magazine and porn?

Yes, 100%. It led the times with drugs, rock and beer.

Earlier in the interview, I asked you if there was an art to getting girls to sleep with you and you stated society made it easy and suggested they were deprogrammed from family values and tradition. Put that aside, is there is an art of being, a way of acting?

Yes, it comes down to mind control through gestures, eye contact, strategic conversations and touching, and making them feel that they will be loved and find happiness if they are with you.

Would you say, women can have that mind control over men?

Yes, especially the left and abused ones?

What do you mean?

Lots of girls who came to me lost their virginity to their boyfriends and dumped right after. I filled their hurt will drugs, alcohol, and after they not only had sex with a lot of my friends, but they had a certain control over the men that wanted them. They could get anything from them just by a glance, a gesture implying that they like them or they could like them.

If I said to you people and society were programmed to be raped with an ideology that penetrated and broke family values and tradition in America, would you call that a conspiracy?

Are you saying I raped these girls?

I am not blaming you for anything, but asking you if the situation in society could have programmed you to make these girls think you loved them, and for the girls to be programmed to be fooled or accept to do things they would not do with a conscious decision?

It was a combination of things. The girl I loved cheated on me, and the society was being completely changed by blasting images, articles and movies that were destroying tradition and the family unit and most of all, a marriage and commitment to one person.

So, in a sense you took the pain of your girlfriend cheating on you on a path that may have hurt a lot of girls?

You could say that, Yes.

214 girls. If you could take it all back and just been with one girl that loved you and stuck with you, and you would never have a chance to have sex with any other girl but the person you loved, what would you choose?

The one. Without a doubt, the one.

Thank You.

Subject Four, 220 Girls from 1976-2019

220 girls, that is a big number, why didn't you stick with one woman?

My wife cheated on me, after that I was done and on a rampage.

How did she cheat on you?

She was hanging out with her male friends from work, and started making friends with men. In my time, that was a big no, no, there was no such things as platonic friends, but the damn TV was just punching that stuff out to her, to her girlfriends, to the entire society.

How did you get 220 more girls to sleep with you?

I made friends with them first. Some because of what I said, what I looked like, rebounds from their husbands or boyfriends, curiosity, my money, my job title, and plain old, sex was in the air.

What do you mean sex was in the air?

The books, articles, media, movies and music in the U.S had completely changed, it was as if they were subliminally putting it all out there, reshaping the traditional concepts of loyalty, love, and marriage. Before; if you slept with a girl and didn't' marry her, the neighborhood would have considered you scheming to take her virginity and not commit to her. I guess it was a form of rape. Now, it was all about having as much sex with as many people as possible. Movies were playing showing men as wife beaters, women feeling good going out with a bunch of men, and reaching people's emotions, imprinting in their minds fantasy that completely destroyed the family unit in America. They were simultaneously pushing out Marxist/Socialist style thought in schools, in the media, the arts, and disregarding that we have fought that system which actually turns usually to a dictatorship bent on violence, oppression, rape, murder, and famine for an entire country like China, Russia, North Korea, etc.

Where did you meet the girls?

Bars, clubs, work, through other girlfriends, social media, and even at the grocery store. A smile, and making light conversation, asking about something to get them talking, making eye contact with certain moves that you are interested in who they are.

Were you interested in who they are?

No.

Did you get to sleep with some, and make them think you wanted to have a relationship with them or marry them?

Yes and No. I felt conflicted after my first wife, you could say, I was tormented and something took over me.

How is your first wife now, is she happy?

She is a wreck, medicated for her mental issues each day and needs wine to numb her senses each night so she can sleep. I think back, if she wasn't influenced by her girlfriends to have the male friends while I was gone on duty, it be a different story. She regrets doing what she did, cheating on me. She keeps on telling me she doesn't know what came over her, keeps on saying something was controlling her, it was the influence of her girlfriends and their opinions on our marriage, etc. It was her decision, that changed our paths, a very bad, selfish and nasty decision.

You said sex was in the air. What are the chances the movies, music, media and articles she and her friends were taking in

broke down her barriers, ultimately her defenses to a sense of decency, and being mentally controlled to do what she did?

You mean brain washed?

I mean, Bio-Digital Social Programming of her mind, and bio-chemistry which caused an automated way of being, that was no longer her or really her own decisions.

Wow, you really hit on something there. But it sounds like science fiction.

Let's say If cell phones and computers can be programmed by taking in frequencies, couldn't the software of a human being, let alone a girl who is not mentally that strong at resisting manipulation? Couldn't your constant downloading to your brain and body with images, videos and articles provoking your emotions and family values damage your operating system and take control of it?

Are you trying to say, the sex in the air, was a program designed by someone in media, in our articles we read, the movies, and music?

What I am saying is, deliberately the Russian Socialist/Communist Regime had operations in the U.S designed to reach the youth, entertainment industry and the education system to subvert the country and they implanted some Marxist professors who influenced the entire education system covertly and penetrated our values. All they had to do was implant these ideas, and put systems in place, and very few people with money and big corporations in Hollywood and media led the wave in sub-conscious automated attempts to destroy the U.S, to a point that a girl is actually Bio-Digitally Social Programmed and raped without her free-willed decision. Instead of using force, they broke into the mind and now with Smart Phones and IoT devices, it makes it easy, as the human brain can easily be controlled by those frequencies pumped out with bio-digital degenerate rape automation software from what I call Rape-Mind. Rape-Mind is infused with content in music, dance, movies, articles and social media that actually harms girls, and all of humanity.

Look at Rap lyrics and the mindset Rap bio-digitally sends to little girls, it's a form of bio-digital rape. In fact, the singers in rock and roll had similar messages but not as nasty as rap. Look back at the girls you were with, weren't they not a program of the movies, magazines and music they took in, like a Playboy? Wasn't a considerable amount of the inner layers of the content they took in promoting in subliminal or direct ways to sleep around, do drugs, and go away from tradition because it is cool and people in tradition were not happy?

You are hitting on something really big here. What you are saying is, that generations of girls have been raped and I am part of the program? That I raped and I was programmed to rape? In essence, I was raped of my life with the cheating of my wife, so I started to rape others? That it was a socialist/Marxist system that was put here by Russian Socialists to rape America?

I am saying more than that. I am saying that your mind is like a software, both your software and hardware were manipulated and controlled with Bio-Digital Social Programming to turn from Virtue to Vice in order to hurt you. Look at the singers, a lot don't have a beautiful voice, and they sexualize themselves and the masses of people with ugly images. The art is no longer by someone who spends years sculpting or painting a masterpiece of beauty, but unskilled people who draw ugly things with sexual overtones. In fact, a lot of the music is by gangsters or thugs, who see women as sexual slaves or objects. When they sing and create tunes and videos, those frequencies are actually bio-digitally imprinting and reprogramming the girls to accept their frequencies, their bio-fields, bio-matter, their state of operating and being; penetrating the listeners defenses, and in turn they get raped by society in a peer environment, or a person under the guise of a hook-up or dating. It is actually similar to how a girl gets kidnapped, raped multiple times, drugged, until she becomes desensitized to it, and sees the rape no longer as rape, but a job or state of being. Those bio-digital messages are actually changing her chemistry and controlling her mind. So, what I am saying is, the culture of humanity has been raped in subtle ways little by little bio-digitally, and it's been completely programmed in people with the invention of the internet and IoT devices that carry Bio-Fields and Bio-Matter.

Let me ask you, were your parents and grandparents happy together in comparison to all your friends and 220 people you had sex with and their friends who had so many sexual partners?

I would say yes 100%, my parents and grandparents were happy and they were loyal to each other.

So, what do you think of the bio-digital social programming to be raped analysis?

I never thought of it that way. But looking back, at my experiences, and hardships I have gone through, and today, I can sit here, and take emotion and interest out of concepts through self-reflection and I would 100% agree with the Bio-Digital Social Programming concept. But, wow, it's really hard to believe. You are saying humanity is not themselves?

I am saying even further. That the news reporters, media, Hollywood, music artists, therapists, all of them are at the same time victims and negative programmed characters of bio-digital social programming from vice that attached to their emotions and bio-chemistry to lead society and hurt girls, families and humanity. The victims are on the left, center and right of the political and social spectrums. Of course, this doesn't excuse their actions, especially if they continue down this path of destroying so many lives through their bio-digitally harmful content that sexualizes girls and spreads subliminal ideas of violent socialism that has hurt billions of people around the world. Everyone is given a brain to self-reflect, and try to be rational, if they fail at that, they will be issued the responsibility somehow by the universe, as there may be a bio-digital code with a certain frequency based on virtue that humanity has been programmed to go against it, at its own detriment and suffering.

Are you saying the world-over is being raped through Bio-Digital Social Programming?

Yes. Not just sexually raped, but in every way that is categorized as vice.

Wow.

So, you are saying people are not themselves, and not free with the freedoms they have?

The laws are free, their actions are free, but their minds and biochemistry have been bio-digitally programmed to fail in the long run through programmed decisions based on vice that is contrary to the program that is healthy and traditional, in turn making an entire society suffer, dependent on mental medication and addicted to drugs, smoking, video games and negative behaviors.

Last question, what is the most powerful form of Bio-Digital Social Programming, Movies, Music, Articles-Books?

For me, Movies.

Thank you.

Subject Five, 250-300 Girls from 1995-2019

How did you manage to sleep with almost 300 girls?

It was all around me. In school, at parties, night clubs, and the number may be a lot more than that, I was on X and other drugs for so many years, and honestly can't remember.

Did you give the impression to girls that you wanted a relationship or they are the only one that you will love, and that you will stay with them?

I loved all of them. I mean, well, yea, some of them cried over me for weeks, I guess I hurt them a lot, I just couldn't commit.

Why? Why couldn't you commit?

I lost my mother when I was young. Actually, she divorced my dad, left us for another man, with her new kids, I didn't see her that much. Reflecting back, I was always afraid to commit and today, I still can't.

Did you offer or influence the girls to do drugs?

Yes, all of them. X, Cocaine, weed and a lot of drinking.

Without the weed, X, cocaine and drinking, do you think you would have slept with 300 girls?

No, may be 10-20.

Because you couldn't use that to influence them, or because those drugs wouldn't have influenced you to hurt so many girls with non-commitment after you slept with them?

Both, but I still wouldn't have reached 300, in fact, the number 300 may not be accurate. I may have slept with 500-800 girls the past 20 years, but lost memory after 300, I was on drugs all the time. So, the 250-300 number is a really low estimate of what I can remember.

What type of music did you play at these events?

Rap, Hip Hop, and some rock, but mostly Rap and Hip Hop.

The first girl you were with, did you want to stay with her?

Yes and No. Part of me wanted to have a good life, the other part was afraid of committing and really wanted to get as many girls as possible. I was addicted to porn, watched VHI, MTV, Howard Stern, had playboy magazines, and everything in the entertainment industry was promoting sex, drugs and the impression it gave you that it was fun and people were happy. But looking back, none of it was fun, and I was never myself.

What do you mean you were never yourself, was it like something led you to be that way?

You can say that; it was as if something led me to do these things. I was in the moment, all the time, and under the influence.

Besides the drugs, media, literature and music that were components, were there any other elements that made it successful for you to get these girls to sleep with you?

Yes. My friends, their friends and social media. It was a system and we all listened to Rap and Hip Hop, some rock, and did the same drugs, and had the same hang outs.

Were your friend's and their friend's girls or boys.

Combination. Usually the girl's girlfriends said good things about me or introduced me through social media, at parties, etc.

What percentage of the girls that cried and were really hurt were virgins?

Almost all of them.

After you did that, sort of hurt their future values of love, did you keep track of what happened to these girls?

Some got really bad, after being hurt, they slept with so many guys, they were used by guys even more like trash, and they got into drugs. Some I don't know, and some got into other relationships, and moved onto another relationship one after another.

If you had a chance to take it all back, and stay with that first one and married her, and never experience the 300-800 girls, would you?

Yes, without a doubt. Today, I am a mess, I need to drink each night, and can't go without smoking weed, and I constantly reflect on what I did and what happened to my life and theirs.

Would you call it manipulation and using techniques for them to open up so they can have sex with you?

Yes.

How is that different from physical rape?

Well, one you physically rape them, the other you sort of get in their mind without them knowing it, in a sense.

Well, isn't that rape by using a different method? As an example I can break into a bank and steal the money physically, I can hack into a bank and digitally transfer the money by programming the software to think it should give me the money based on a commitment to hold it or utilize it for a scheduled period and later the system is corrupted or throws red flags wondering why it transferred the money.

Hm, I never thought of it that way. It's very complex. Lot of factors.

Well, you mentioned drugs, drinking, music, social media, and friends. Well, I have another question, let's say if you and some of your friends knew at a subconscious level that you were influencing or training the girls, would you consider that the ideology from the imagery, music, movies, articles, magazines, with the combination of drugs and drinking programmed you to program them?

Wow. That's deep. You mean I was subliminally programmed to rape the girls, and your definition of rape is using emotional techniques, with certain music and drugs to get them to drop their defenses, is rape, but not in an old school way of physically forcing them?

Yes, and I am adding to it. What I mean is, your mind and your biochemistry was bio-digitally social programmed, and was on automation mode to varying degrees, as were the girls. And this penetration, started at full force in the 1950's, and it is full blown now with the Internet, IoT, Smart Phones and AI. Peoples culture, mind, and decision making are almost

completely controlled by computers and bad behavior that has hurt humanity, and is actually leading to hurt it even more.

1950's, who?

You can look it up, it was Communist/Socialist spies from Russia that infiltrated and social programmed just a few movie producers, newspapers, and entertainment company owners, and they led the wave of destruction to step by step ruin not only America, but the entire world. Almost everyone has been Bio-Digitally Social Programmed to be involved in it. Karl Marx ideology took the lead in this.

If you said this to me 20 years ago, I would have cursed at you and thought you were nuts, but looking back, at all my mistakes, the suffering I caused the girls and myself, it really makes sense. Wow. I don't know about the Russian Socialist part though, but wow, yea, I feel what you're saying about the Bio-Digital Social Programming. Why Socialism?

Because the forerunners of socialism were promoting everything that has gone against tradition, the family and contributed to not only the death of 150 million people around the world in the 20th century, but the emotional anguish of so many young girls that were Raped through Bio-Digital Social Programming in the U.S and Europe, and now it has spread to Japan, China and all over the Spanish world and even India and Africa.

But, you are pretty much saying I was a rapist without realizing I was, and it's a form of rape, a really super clever form of rape?

I am saying everyone is a victim of this Bio-Digital Social Programming from Marxist/Socialist ideologies that has hurt so many people and raped a lot of girls, and ruined families and the entire society. That is what I am saying. This form of Bio-Digital Social Programming is absolutely rape at its most sophisticated

form rooted from what I call Rape-Mind that used Bio-Digital Hybrid Sexual Assault techniques.

Damn, that is genius in a way, and in a way, I am, I'm sorry about everything I ever did, and I kind of understand it more now.

Do you think, like cell phones or computers, a human being has a sort of software or a brain that can be programmed remotely?

Hm. How Remotely?

Well, all you need is an internet connection to download or upload something in terms of computers. Well, what if that same internet works the same way on humans as you download things when you hear, see or touch them, yet you are not consciously aware of it? And That downloading can have a complex automation operating system. If its vice and harmful, it can hurt you.

Very Interesting. You are saying like computers we have a hardware and software?

Yes, and one more component computers or AI does not have.

What is that?

That's another, deep and long discussion that I will have in section 3 of my book. My point here is, like computers, virus's and malware and reprogramming software have been sent to people since the 1950's in mass, and in real digital form since the invent of computers, and smart phones. In fact, smart phones make you a cyborg, and it controls you Bio-Digitally.

How are girls a part of this thing, meaning if men were the rapists, what is their role? You can't blame all men?

Not at all, at the beginning girls were mainly the victims, then the Bio-Digital Social Programming started using them against men. It is like a virus that corrupts the system. Lots of men have also been hurt as well. Entrapped by women who used them for money, their belongings, and made them feel like they were truly loved. And this stems largely from broken homes and broken families. Before, it was different, even if you didn't love someone, there was values, integrity, respect, loyalty, and responsibility that kept marriages together. My point here, is the entire culture is at fault for this and this bio-digital social programming inputted by Socialist Spies from Russia is not just about rape, it's about the destruction and interconnectivity of everything to form a Communist global system that is authoritarian. Everyone has added to this without being aware.

To end this, I have one final question for you. What do you think is the strongest Bio-Digital Social Programming Tool, Music, Movies, or Articles?

For me, Music.

Thank you...

SECTION TWO

The Beginning of Rape in History with Physical Force VS the Invisible Force of Today
Rape in History

Usually rapes happened when an invading army won the war, enslaved the population, and raped the men's wives, daughters and families.

War World II, The Socialist-Communist Regime of Russia

The Russian Socialist Regime and their red soldiers raped roughly 2 million German-Austrian girls, and women from the ages of 8-80 years old in the span of just 2 years. Children's orphanages, schools, churches and family residence were rape grounds for the Socialist Regime's Gang Rapes of grandmothers, mothers and daughters that continued daily. Many boys died defending their sisters and mothers as they watched them raped by the Socialist Red Army. The raping went on night and day reaching millions of people, even some Jews, polish and Ukrainian girls were victims of the Socialist Army.

The Invading Mongols Raped Millions of People in the Persian, Arab and Roman Lands

Old Persian Oral Traditions that have written historical records archived from the 13th century have a quote from Genghis Khan and the invading Mongols. *"The greatest pleasures for a man, is to defeat his enemy, possess what they have, exterminate them, watch their wives and daughters cry, and ride their behinds, to take their princesses, and concubines as pillows, to look upon them, kiss their shiny faces, suck their lips and fruit colored nipples"*

The Mongol invasion and raping continued for hundreds of years of one Khan's rule after another mainly in the Persian-Iranian regions which includes modern Iran--Afghanistan, and modern-day Turkey, until later there were not many indigenous blonde-haired blue-eyed Persians left and many Arabs were massacred. The rest got mixed with marriages from 1500-2000AD. The Mongol rapes ended what the Invading Caliphate could not finish 2 centuries prior. In fact, today, the Iranian people do not even realize it, but the word Mr. has turned to Khan, and Ms. to Khanum, all derived from the Mongolian word for Ruler, Khan. The rape is deeply ingrained in their culture, minds, and language, and that reinforces their cultural sensitivies to wear the clothes to an extreme, as they experienced one invasion after another starting from Alexander the Great, the Arabs, and Mongols.

"The Mongols came, drove off rich nobles and scholars to the woods. They sieged the city, separated the men from the women, and ravished their virgin daughters and sisters"

Looking at today's Persian Language, it comprises mainly of words rooted in German, Arabic and Mongolian-Chinese, attesting to the historical rape invasions and to the Chinese and Greek Historical accounts of what Persian/Iranian's looked like, their language and customs prior to being invaded. Linguists would describe them as Indo-European, but someone who is very educated in language and history, would see that it is a combination of Indo-European, Altaic and Semitic languages which sound Arabic-Hebrew, German, Chinese and Mongolian.

In 2500 BC, the Persian empire had around 30 recognized ethnicities, allowing diversity, abolishment of slavery, and freedoms similar to the U.S constitution protecting choice in customs, religion, and human rights as attested by the Cyrus Cylinder, the oldest known declaration of human rights displayed at the U.N. Headquarters. The diversity and human rights afforded to people, were destroyed through multiple invasions from 336bc, around 650AD, and 1250AD. Some structures carried themes very close to Socialism that attached to the invading platforms that decimated the human rights given to the people by Cyrus the Great. In fact, those rights, spawned many books from Xenophon such as "Cyropaedia", and books describing methods of rule and government that are rooted in the American Constitution. The founding fathers were greatly inspired by them. Cyrus the Great had gone against the grain, of the old oral tradition "to the victors go the spoils". Meaning, you can rape and take what you want. After Alexander, Cyrus's ideas of human rights and rule, largely disappeared through the emerging empires.

Mass Rapes through war were committed by Romans, Greeks, Jews, Persians, Arabs, Egyptians, English, Chinese, Mongolians, Japanese, Indians and African Tribes throughout history. All of humanity is guilty of it. Throughout history, only a sense of chivalry, human decency, or fear of God curtailed rape during war or the aftermath during the time of foreign rule. Now it is different, we are facing world-wide rape, human trafficking and sex trafficking without realizing how it actually works, and how it can be remedied.

Today: 20th-21st Century Rape VIA Bio-Digital Social Programming: Invasion by Marxist/Socialist Methods

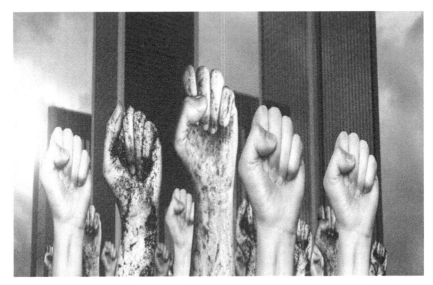

to Attack Culture Rooted in Family Ethics

20th century began a New era of invisible Marxists/Socialist Armies using Bio-Digital Social imprinting and Bio-Digital Hybrid Sexual Assault Programming to rape an entire society through altering its moral/ethical values to take over its assets and hurt girls far and wide.

A concrete ideological plan was installed in the United States by the Communist Government of Russia to implant soft methods of brainwashing society through the education system, media and movies. One by one, they implanted spies, corrupting ideas and divisive influence through music, dance, literature, movies and schools in order to penetrate the family unit, and break the U.S.A. The goal was to stop America's efforts in fighting communism's enslavement of people around the globe and the developing global socialist platforms predicated by Marxists. Most people who fled Communism-Socialism, wished to immigrate to the U.S.A. The majority of immigrants have fled to America from the hurt and misery caused by the destructive socialist platforms created in their own country by violent socialist revolutionaries.

Early 1900's Socialist Marxist Thought led to Rape and Murder of Millions in Russia

Lenin, Trotsky, and the Socialist's took advantage of the people's disdain for war, and created a murderous revolution that took over the government, murdered the royal family and countless people. They urged for the destruction of family values, ethics and morals as espoused by Karl Marx's violent ideals for a social revolution which led to famine and countless other murders. Women and men were encouraged not to marry, and not to raise families, rather to sleep around, drink to access, commit porn acts, view pornography, and attack faith-based people. It ended with the Socialist Dictator, Stalin, who murdered millions more.

Advertisement Promoting Rape and Sexual Revolution through Socialism in Russia 1915-1920's

There were posters in Russia that read "Each Communist male can and should satisfy his sexual urge and every Communist female must aid him". Sexual violence became an epidemic, and rape of former bourgeois women and noble women was considered class justice. Sex education became mandatory for the youth and school kids, while STD's were rampant. People traded their traditional Russian attire that attested to the diversity in each region, to Communist Uniforms and baring it all to be provocative. The sexualization of the people who aligned with Socialism was deeply ingrained in the boys and girls of Socialist Armies that were later termed by historians as "An Army of Rapists". There are accounts from every Soviet occupied territory around the world, of the Socialist Armies rapes, reaching all the way to the Caucasus regions, not just the German territory in the aftermath of WWII.

1920-30's Socialism/Communist in Germany

Karl Marx's violent Socialist/Communist movement, promotion of sexualization of girls, sex education and pornography were widespread and promoted by the Socialist's as a weapon to break the family, and take over the state in Germany. The Socialist platforms and violent struggles in the streets contributed greatly to division in Germany, that influenced the formation of WWII.

1900-1950's Socialism in the U.S and The Rise to Sexualization of Girls

Socialism with the aid of German and Russian Socialists took some root in America. Socialists Bombed Wallstreet and sent a number of mail bombs to prominent American businesses and government leaders. Prior to that, President Wilson curtailed them, and after the violent acts of socialists, President Hoover and President Roosevelt utilized the U.S Constitution, treason laws and the FBI to stop any advancement towards overpowering Americas democracy and freedoms with Socialisms authoritarian systems.

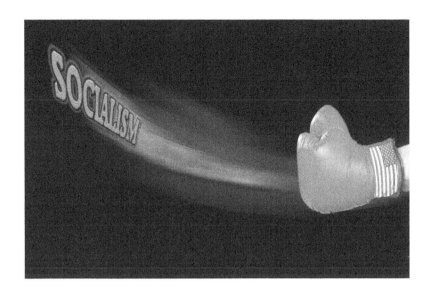

Internal Documents of the FBI

ANTIFIA (Socialists) violent acts and financial sabotage contributed to the depression in America. When the Socialists

failed at forming a violent revolution in the U.S, the Socialists turned to culture and sexualizing of the youth under the banner of freeing the sexually deprived and oppressed. The FBI and the U.S government had internal documents with concerns that Moscow's 5th column, or Violent Socialists were being funded and supported through TV, Radio, Screen VIA Hollywood, Broadway, and our major newspapers and making their way into the academic institutions in order to indoctrinate the youth in universities, and spread hatred towards the U.S.A in Europe, the Balkans, Asia, Africa and Moscow. Internal CIA and FBI documents warned that Socialists aimed to create a global Socialist/Communist System that can control the masses, bringing tyranny, misery, and death for the worlds people.

Because America's Constitution and governmental checks and balances system was structured in a brilliant way that was different from anywhere else on the planet, it was almost impossible to subvert the U.S in the short run. Hence a Social Programming campaign to destroy the family unit and sexualize young girls and the youth began as they did in Russia before the mass murders, as they began a campaign to teach little kids about sex.

Violent Socialism didn't happen overnight in the U.S as it did in Russia killing millions and raping untold women, and even some men. The Bio-fields behind the American political system and government is almost impenetrable, lest the majority of society becomes socialist through bio-digital social programming and the U.S is on the verge of civil war with a great deal of its assets owned by foreign powers, with the populous operating in a state of sexualization, and the youth taking their freedoms for granted leading to unrest and revolution after socialism takes control of government. We do face this danger now to varying degrees.

1953 Alfred Kinsey Socialist Theory of Sexualization

Alfred Kinsey interviewed prostitutes, child molesters, rapists, and sexually frustrated people to create his data pool. He used that to spread the message that the youth should watch porn, made implications of child sex, and to sleep around, and all kinds of sexual behavior are okay, and people shouldn't be so hasty to marry and have kids. Newspapers and the TV started to blast his findings which stemmed from Socialist thought. Teachers and researchers started to replicate his finding that were rooted with subjects who were rapists and prostitutes. Society started to change. Next was the coming of *Playboy* Magazine.

1953 to Now
Playboy

Playboy used a symbol that most little kids and girls would relate to and find harmless. A bunny, and its tail, and stuck it on the behinds of young voluptuous girls from broken homes and families, took images of them, and sold their bodies through print so men and boys can, not only watch them and sexually fantasize about multiple girls, but replicate the behavior throughout society.

The visual and written narratives of the magazine was led by a vision of a bachelor life, and the attacks on marriage, the family and ethics that kept girls safe from rape. This was the vision of its founder, after his wife cheated on him, and he took the hurt into his magazine that demoralized an entire nation.

Strategically, through mainly subconscious automation, the founder of *Playboy* highjacked and used the female and black civil rights movements and the war era, to its advantage, which spawned multiple competing magazines, and industry's that used the same formula that changed the obscenity laws that prevented sexualization of young girls, which transitioned to the degrading of women in the porn industry.

They were able to beat the FBI and bio-digitally social program the jury for a win. The family values that existed for the majority of people in the U.S, were replaced with the values of just a few people who came from broken marriages and broken families, and addicted to drugs, which hurt a lot of people.

Penthouse

Penthouse used the term Pet, to describe its Playmates as promoted by *Playboy*. *Penthouse*, took pictures of young girls naked, called them pets, and sold them to men all over. It was a new form of slavery, as before, slaves may have been considered human beings, but now, girls were likened in subliminal ways as animal pets you can imagine having sex with one after another, do as you wish with them and share them.

Porn

Porn showed women as nothing but sexual products to be used in nasty ways. It implied and promoted a vision that resembled a world where you can really hurt a girl, how to degrade her, treat her like a nasty beast. It was a modern form of prostitution where an entire society gets involved.

Someone pays someone to have sex, and the entire society pays to fantasize about their sex by watching them like perverts. Porn became the modern form of slavery and prostitution involving an entire society's support from viewership or complicity to its existence. Moreover, it led to a very nasty automated rape system imbedded in the human culture, replicating bio-digitally in people's bodies, addicting them and creating rape automation, and software that engages in Hybrid-Bio-Digital Sexual Assault through Bio-Digital Social Programming. In fact, the imagery and videos, create a bio-digital connection with human beings, that replicates in huge numbers in their body and brain, affecting and intermingling with every decision they make in society in unseen ways. Their bio-fields were infected. Bio-Digital Social Programming, Hybrid Bio-Digital Sexual Assault, Replication, Bio-Digital Fields, Bio-Matter and Rape Mind will be discussed with detail in section 3.

Socialist Hijacking of the Black Movement for Freedom

After interviewing many prominent Black Americans in the U.S, the common message was:

"Rape is not a representative of our Black-American culture".

One prominent businessman said *"Rap is a stain on our African-American heritage. The culture of our slave masters, the way they talked, their total lack of humanity, somehow moved onto these youth, and is destroying Black people and our culture in a way slavery could not. When we were slaves, you could take and corrupt our bodies, but you couldn't take our minds, you could never take our soul, our heritage. Now the soul of the Black man has been taken, and fed the illusion of money, fame, and sex, this is not where we came from"*

Another said, The Socialists hijacked our Black movement for freedom. Playboy, dirty singers, and musicians, and entertainer's, hijacked our black movement, picked gang bangers and a lot of hateful uneducated people to put in the entertainment industry, and they corrupted our daughters, and our sons and used that for their own political movements, trying to say hundreds of years of slavery and abuse is the same for their little causes of socialism, and equal rights. They used us, and used clever little words in their speeches to ride the wave of freedom upon the black wave of justice."

Socialism made the Black mind think they should be dependent on their government, rather their family, community and take advantage of the American Constitution to build their own path.

SECTION THREE
Bio-Digital Social Programming

Bio-Digital Social Programming uses emotions, culture, touch, sound, sight, voice and proximity of bio-digital fields and bio-matter with written words, movies, music, and dance to social program a person or an entire society with a replicating software that uses bio-matter as a way to attack, and connect through the internet and the Human Bio-Digital Network with the aid of a human body, machines, computers, smart phones, smart cities, IoT devices, Facial Recognition and Artificial Intelligence.

How most people are Infected by a Bio-Digital Virus called Rape-Mind through the Bio-Digital Human Network?

The Human Bio-Digital Network

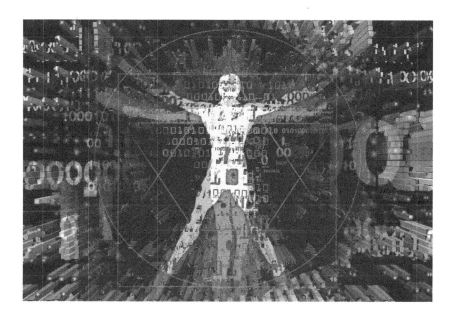

There is the internet, and there is what I have discovered through technologies similar to AI, The-Bio-Digital Network for human's and any life form that is not made from machines. I have coined this network as The Human Bio-Digital Network, or The Bio-Digital Human Network. In fact, this bio-digital network can connect with frequencies through people and objects, regardless of distance.

Much like the internet, where information is transferred from one machine to another in very fast and unseen ways, human beings and non-machines actually connect bio-digitally in mostly unconscious ways. This bio-digital connection can be made not only with people, but with content displayed in writing, in an image, video or in certain proximities of things and objects.

Machines can connect through the internet via IoT devices, computers, robots, and smart phones. People can connect through the bio-digital human network, and the internet. The issue is, about 70% of their brain is locked up, or completely untapped. Hence, any connection they make, is mostly unconscious and they are part of the programming and have hardly any free will because their thoughts are a product of the bio-digital social programming they received through the bio-digital human network as well as the internet.

Rape-Mind

Rape-Mind is a Bio-Digital Programming Software that enters people and objects through the Global Bio-Digital Network, Internet and the Human Bio-Digital Network as Rape-Mind carries bio-fields that put out Bio-Matter with codes that read in the same lines of Destruction, Termination and Rape. Rape-Minds Bio-Digital Fields sends out Bio-Matter to everything via Replication of its own identity and Bio-Digital Field and Malevolent Bio-Matter. Rape Mind is basically hacking and reprograming of your brain with a digital brain in the sub-layers of your existing brain. Rape-Mind can enter and connect with you via Smart Phones, Robotics, Smart Cities, Smart Homes, Haptic Suits, and be exponentially effective in reprogramming you via virtual reality, augment reality, mixed reality and holograms.

Bio-Digital Field

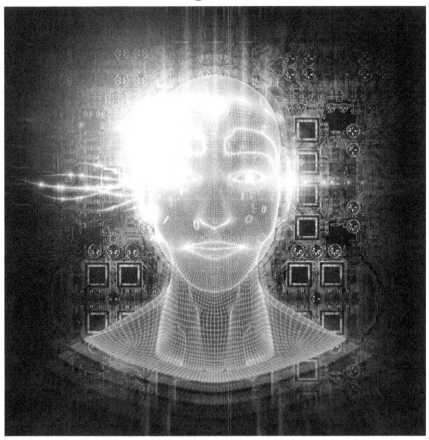

Each person carries a bio-digital field that through the combination of multiple bio-metric tools can be discerned of its quality, energy potency, health, intelligence, thoughts and character. It consists of people's genetic make-up, bio-digital social programming experiences, their innate digital or conscious unique self, developing thoughts, intent, frequencies and bio-matter that is entering them or expelling from them via the Human Bio-Digital Network, bio-fields in their cells, microscopic elements, their flesh, skin receptors, eyes, ears, and all vital organs. All of those combined can make a comprehensive bio-field that surrounds the person's body from 1 inch, to those who have huge bio-digital field spheres that can shoot out frequencies through touch, eye, and skin receptors. 99.9 percent of the people cannot do this, and those who usually can, do it at a sub-conscious level. The 99.9 percent fall into the category of a very weak proximity bio-digital field that surrounds their body in low frequencies. However, robots, can be programmed to extract frequencies, redirect frequencies and send bio-digital frequencies much like a smart phone that received a picture or a video from 10,000 miles away in a matter of mere seconds. This can be done with AI Automation. Bio-Fields can be implanted by an AI system, to replicate itself within your own bio-digital field until it becomes a part of all of your bio-digital field exerting influence and control over all of your cells, organs, and finally your digital brain. This is done through Rape-Mind's software that acts similar to a malware and virus. If Rape-Mind in infused with Lewd, and Pornographic content, the persons bio-digital field will continuously replicate Rape-Minds software and content, to form the person's thoughts, actions and identity rooted in Rape-Mind. Their Bio-Digital field and bio-metric readings will all display the Rape-Mind content.

Bio-Matter

Bio-Matter has the intrinsic qualities of a person's bio-digital field or sphere. Whether healthy, sick, good, bad, intelligent, capable, evasive, kind, patient, and honest. Basically, codes that translate to virtue and vice are in bio-fields that get transmitted through bio-matter that contains that message and bio-digital quality. Bio-Matter can be sent via a smart phone, IoT device, computer, robot, the internet, the human Bio-Digital Network and through the absorption, touch and sending of bio-matter in virtual reality, augmented reality, and mixed reality with holograms.

Bio-Fields & Bio-Matter Transmit Through All Avenues

Bio-fields and bio-matter through the eye, voice, speech, touch, smell, and all electronic forms of text, email and digital messages carry over a person's, or networks bio-digital fields and its contents. For example, when you receive a text, based on its sentence structure, and situation, you may feel or know what the person is thinking or planning next. However, some people with that gut intuition can know and feel even if the sentence structure and wording is off topic. This information is transmitted to their brain via sub-conscious automation from their different organs and senses as it forms a thought and gut feeling inside their mind. This is because the persons conscious thoughts, sub-conscious thoughts and un-conscious thoughts, and all the layers of bio-fields in every organ, skin receptor and brain contribute to the formation of the text message from the sending party, while the receiving party has the same innate capability to absorb that digital message and content. An animal has instinctive senses as well, but they don't operate like human's do, as their digital network are very limited compared to the Human Bio-Digital Network.

How Sexual Neural Circuits are Bio-Digitally Programmed like a Virus into You to Rape or be Raped

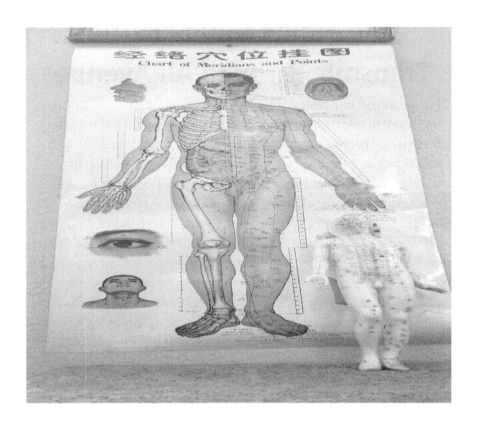

The Chinese, Indians and some other civilizations have maps of the human body that are similar with today's modern maps of the nervous system and circulatory system. These maps date back almost 2000 years.

In Chinese, they are called meridian channels, acupuncture points, etc. These channels not only can travel vertically, but connect in crisscross, diagonal, spiral and circulatory patters. There is a channel that is connected with your private parts and your brain, and parts of your body that have sexual or sensual sensations with touch, sound or visual simulation and as an example can easily get activated with movies you watch or music you listen to. These channels can carry information through uploads or downloads similar to a computer, via touch, sound or through your eyes.

The contents that travel through your meridian channels or neuropathways can create a continuous automated cycle of replication. Even the contents that comprise of the individual's character, biochemistry and thought process can be transferred to you to varying degrees.

One of the biggest strongest channels are related to sex organs, and they can be manipulated, and reprogrammed, and sent through other organs that circulate back to the brain, that eventually creates a circulatory pattern that is automated with the information it took in.

For example, playboy magazine's depiction of girls as sexual objects, and the founder's actual brain and its view on the girls got transferred into the individual boys and men who viewed the images, read his articles and watched his shows. This more so is the case for porn and the type of people who created them. It is Rape-Mind that can bio-digitally transfer onto another person.

There is a channel that goes from the eye, down through the cheeks, raps around the side of the ear, down your tongue and throat, through all the vital organs, and connects with your penis or vaginal area, and circulates around your extremities, fingers, back through key areas in the brain. That channel actually creates a bio-energy center with content stored in the private parts of the body, with pathways ready to activate on demand with external stimuli that enters the eyes and ears or by touch and certain proximities with other Bio-Fields. In fact, there are brain storage centers not only in the human brain, but in our organs and even our skin has it.

Our body can actually connect with the internet just like IoT, Smart Phones and Electronic Devices, it's just that people don't know how to tap into certain areas of the brain and open the 100,00 channels that can exist in the human body. The opening of these channels is actually regulated by a code in the body. I call this code the Bio-Digital System Code, which is regulated and governed by elements that relate to virtue, instead of Vice that have a property programmed in the Human Bio-Digital Network.

The point is, people can be and have been programmed to rape in automated ways by having their software or channels reprogrammed or corrupted, to the detriment of themselves. The entire society has received this programming. Anyone operating a computer, TV, or smart phone has received this programming, affecting the whole society, in a matrix of infinite ways. If a computer can get a digital virus or malware or be programmed, so can the human software that actually attaches to the channels that regulate and are connected with human emotion and sensory perception.

Rape-Mind Registers in Bio-Digital Codes Measured via Your Biometrics, Coding & Human Bio-Digital Network

Peoples thoughts, intentions and actions can be predicted, detected and influenced through incorporating a hybrid of bio-metric tools. Facial recognition can detect your emotions, and to certain degrees your thoughts and actions. Skin detection tools can analyze your health. Voice, word type and sentence pattern detection tools can

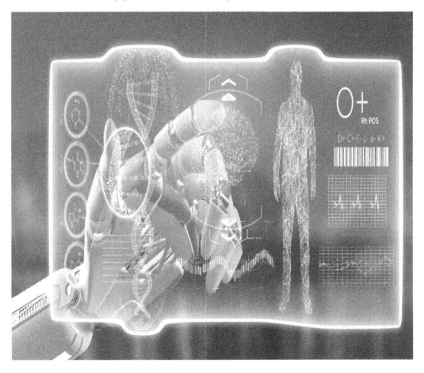

analyze your thoughts, intent and character. Human detection tools can detect your skeleton, muscles, gestor, pose and internal organs.

Facial Recognition

Facial recognition can be uses to scan through thousands of pre-recorded criminal faces, and use that data with AI to scan other people in search of previously unidentified criminals, sex offenders, rapists, murderers, etc. In essence, this technique and tool can be used to find people before they commit their next crime, and identify people who have already committed crimes.

Brain & Vocal Cord Signal Interception Device & Software

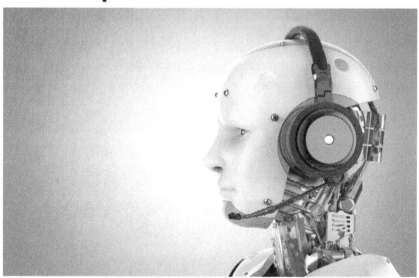

This device created not only by MIT, but other institutions, and corporations, can intercept electrical signals that your brain sends to your vocal cords and transmit your information to a computer. The device is currently wearable; however, tech companies and the Chinese military are investing in programs that can allow it to be installed in robots and implanted in heads of human beings so that they be powered by AI and have access and control to the internet autonomously. If machines can do this, do humans actually do it at sub-conscious and un-conscious levels? We discovered they actual do via The Human Bio-Digital Network

Thought Detection Device & Software to Extract Brain Data

The detection software can detect brain signals from outside the human skull, using laser's and fiber optics to measure blood flow, with the combination of facial, voice and many other technologies, to decipher your exact thoughts from a distance. A lot of our research and development used technology and techniques as we were connecting with the Human-Bio-Digital Network to scan, detect, and decode people and Rape-Mind.

Infection of your Bio-Digital Field with Porn, & Lewd Content that Replicates in Your body, Brain and Mind as Rape-Mind

Facial Recognition and Porn

We have discovered that people who watch porn, and are addicted to porn, can be detected with an AI system in some facial recognition software. There are systems similar but more efficient than the present technological aspects of AI, that actually can penetrate the human bio-field and the human skin, and see the replicating process of the porn people watch. It's actually harming the human body, its cells, and health and creating a disturbed bio-digital mind, prone to rape automation at an almost conscious level. This mind, I have termed, Rape-Mind, as its patterns produce codes like an invading virus, that replicates until it eliminates its host.

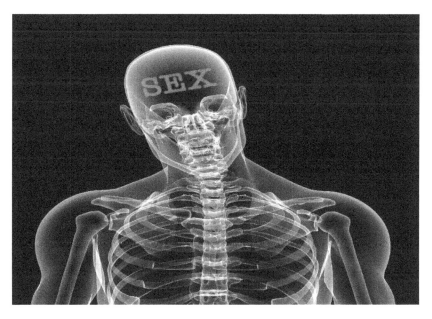

Characters such as Alfred Kinsey, some Porn Stars, Rapists, some rappers, some rock stars, pop stars, and murderous Socialist Dictators such as Stalin, Mao, Lenin, Trotsky, Castro and convicted child molesters all have the same Rape-Mind bio-field within their Facial Recognition building blocks. That bio-field replicates itself after entering other human's bio-fields through bio-digital content they take in, colliding with their cells and DNA which has a pre-built defense mechanism to content that is vice and harmful to its health. However, the replicating process, much like virus's and malware take their tole, through complicit socialist perspectives of society, a constant barrage of degenerate lewd content via entertainment, and bio-digital social programing with peers, or society at large.

Emotional Programming via Bio-Digital Programming with Un-Conscious, Sub-Conscious and Conscious Rape Automation of Girls

The emotion of love, or sexual desire, can and has been influenced throughout human history, to convince oneself or another to come together, to commit, to build something special, as it has to betray, steal, kill, and destroy. Lewd, and degenerate content, from a mind that is perverted, selfish, greedy, disloyal, and completely negative, and ingenuine in character, has penetrated the entire societies imagery, art, movies, music, education, books and articles. The mind, has achieved rape-mind automation in society.

Rape Automation

Pretending to be your Friend or wanting to be your friend in order to manipulate your emotions and gain your trust to have sex with you, is a form of rape, that is in fact almost an automated process in society, in people's minds, and even in their very cells that has turned to rape automation.

In history, you made vows to respect, cherish, love, and be loyal to one person after a courtship, or an introduction attesting to each other's characters and virtues. In society today, people have been programmed to scheme into attracting the opposite sex, manipulating their emotions, to achieve sex or other objectives and move on the next person, fooling themselves and others.

It is not only men who have done this to women, women have and are doing this to men as well to obtain different things they may want, including the automated sex program that has enslaved their operating system, or in human words, their heart and mind. Unfortunately, both have been programmed to hurt each other and the entire society, and all of humankind.

Rape Automation at Universities, Parties, Clubs and Social Encounters

A young boy, may act, say, do, go, touch or imply to a girl, in an almost automated programmed way while at school, in a party, a club, or any social encounter to manipulate or get ahead in one way, in order to social program the girl and create a situation in a place, that her decision is no longer hers, but the automated process that triggers bio-digital responses in her mind and body.

Some of this rape is unconscious rape automation, that is completely instinctual, but in the past, it was regulated by societies cultural laws and obscenity laws that kept the bad in check. Some of this rape component is subconscious and some is conscious rape automation. Music and Video content at sports games, cheerleading, sororities, dance clubs and so on, all of these are programming and promoting the rape of girls, and sex for all in an automated way through Bio-Digital Social Programming with Rape-Minds Bio-Digital Hybrid Sexual Assault.

Un-Conscious Rape Automation

In an unconscious rape automation, the automated program to get the girl, is completely benign to the man, as they are both going through the motions. But it's emotions, regulated through circuits that connect to not only the private parts in a sexual way, but in different organs, in particular the heart, stomach and kidneys are actually completely controlled by the content it received on what and how sex should be, and how it should be obtained through TV, Music, Dance, literature or human contact. If the content received contained bio-digital elements of Porn, Nude demeaning photos, sexually explicit content via literature, all coming from a creator's Rape-Mind that is completely different from the traditional family approach to courtship, as most of their creators of the sexual revolution were, then this creates a subconscious rape automation system within humanity. The unconscious rape automation is rare, as most people, have a side, that is aware.

Sub-Conscious Rape Automation

Subconscious Rape Automation is the king. Most people have a knowing side, deep down, they know what is good and bad, and what can hurt people. The issue is, after the 1950's, peoples Bio-Digital Software was corrupted with porn, drugs, disloyalty, non-commitment, and lewd acts that have actually penetrated their very cells and gone against every ounce that made the family unit.

A constant barrage of Bio-Digital Social Programming that originated from socialism and men whose minds were built to sexualize, enslave, and dehumanize women, and break the family unit through Marxist Socialism, are almost in every layer of visual and audio transmissions within all major music, tv, art, education and everything anti-traditional and anti-family culture, we see, hear, and touch. Music, by rappers, make implications of rape, and sublimely program girls to accept it. Prior to that, rock and roll artists and their characters did the same in a different way by just tapping into emotions interrelated to sexual desire.

Now, a swarm of elements, work in sub-conscious automated ways, and like the internet, move in and out of people's bio-digital fields programming people varying in time and degree. This will be further explained in the sections of Smart phones, IoT devices and Bio-Fields.

Most unconscious rape automation, does have elements of ingenuine words, deeds, actions, and implications in order to manipulate or have sex with a girl, or for a girl to entrap a man in a relation. The bio-digital operation, remains at its strongest in the unconscious and subconscious realms.

And yes, there are some people, who consciously understand the way of manipulation and how this works in an almost covert military like operation, but not being smart enough to understand the bio-digital aspects of it. To add to it, they lack the wisdom to know how much harm they are causing to their own bodies and minds, not to mention to their victims.

Conscious Rape Automation

Someone with a conscious rape automation, is completely aware of what he is doing. Through conscious fake smiles, fake words, ingenuine deeds, he or she attempts, manipulates and wins the battle to penetrate a girl's bio-digital field, and rapes her by putting her in a sub-conscious to unconscious rape automated state. Next her bio-digital field is immobilized, and is connected to him, the environment and his bio-digital field that is operating inside of her, which in turn corrupts her system by taking advantage of not only the channels/circuits linked to her emotions, but the sexual circuits connected with her mind, skin receptors, sexual organs, and other organs not related to sexual reproduction.

To add to it, guilt, and a sense of being owned, can predominate the girls will. The rape is further achieved, or sustained through societal acceptance of lewd acts and lewd imagery, peer gossip, as well as its assault on family and traditional culture that has historically taught to respect a girl and a man in a pure virtuous way rather than vice. Moreover, this dumbs down her will, conditions, and reprograms the girl to depend more on the attention and false sense of reward it gets from dancing in a foolish video, (which involves lewd dances), than the attention they are supposed to get from their own families.

IoT, Computers, and Electronic Devices

Your Smart Phones, Computers, TV, Mini Robot Assistants, and any device that connects to your biometric system of voice, sound and touch, can and does influence and reprogram your software to not only be dependent on the connection, but be led by the programming connected with the IoT devices and linked with programming inside the IoT devices.

Sexual Bio-Digital Social Programming through IoT and Apps

Because the content travels through the IoT devices, and the IoT device is strongly linked with your Bio-Digital field, your defenses, free-will and mind are even more likely to accept content that is vice, and bad for your inner being, for your life, for your family and society.

The content, is more easily programmed into you, and constantly replicates, and strengthens its own operating system layer by layer without you realizing it, until you have an emotion or instinctual desire to do something or follow a path you normally would not follow. In essence, you are being conditioned and sexually programmed through bio-digital social programming and its connection through the human bio-digital network, the internet, IoT devices and Apps.

Rap Music Registered High Frequencies & Building Blocks of Rape-Mind

We used a combination of voice, word choice, sentence, facial, body, gesture, lidar and other devices, while connected to the

Human Bio-Digital Network. Rap music frequently spiked to 99.9% displaying multiple characteristics of Rape-Mind. We then looked at its building blocks, the codes registers and translated into frequencies that matched Rape-Mind and Destruction 100%. We then decoded the coding behind its creation, they populated human words such as rape, murder, drugs, hate, revenge, and destruction. The words that populated were not derived from the words spoken by the rappers, rather bio-metric and bio-digital frequencies as they were replicating in the rapper's brains and being sent out to the listener and viewer.

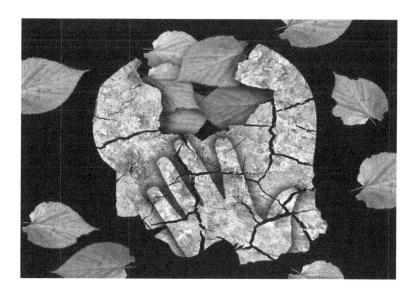

10-15-Year-Old Girls Dancing to Apps that Rappers with Rape-Mind/Sexual Minds Influenced or Created

There are video apps that people dance to and post on Facebook, YouTube and other social media, which gets likes, comments, and connects with other boys, girls, men, families and full on rapists. This can lead her to be sex trafficked and murdered at worst, or be sexualized and enter the rape automation world, lose her virginity through bio-digital social programing, and sleep with one guy after another, and then fall into drugs and getting STDs rather than being brought up to live a fulfilling life with a good man.

Girls Bio-Digitally Programmed with Lewd Content from Women Pop and R&B Singers that have Rape Automation Acceptance Minds in their Voice, and Gesture Outputs

Famous female singers who have been Sexually Bio-Digitally Social Programmed to be lewd, and accept all kinds of sexual behavior such as: sleeping around with risky lifestyles that lead to sexual diseases, emotional issues that need medication and drugs, are bio-digitally sending out to the public their own lewd software, particularly to young girls and boys, and then conditioning them through sight, voice and gesture automation.

A swing of the butt here, a cleavage there, or dark demented gestures that show a disturbed mind, with ugly troll like customs, are bio-digitally programming young girls, and conditioning them to have that imprinting in their software. The performers mind's and bio-fields have already been bio-digitally social programmed by a rapist or lewd male mind, to be a sex slave or be a sexualized entity, rather than achieve success and self-identity through their virtues. That mind is rooted in Rape-Mind that moves through a Socialist Platform

In fact, the mind of the performer, gets implanted into the person who receives the frequencies, much like a cyber-attack, and that mind replicates in the person without their knowledge, corrupting their bio-digital software step by step, little by little. This corruption puts their system on automation mode, but the corrupted software system, much like a virus, controls their brain to actually fight against this awareness and opposition to its existence or any claims that it is being harmful to humanity, girls, boys, and adults all over.

Because, a Bio-digital Rape-Mind, has been created in the human body, by penetrating its bio-digital field, it leads its choices and attempts to resist its deprogramming with comments such as "you are prude, its freedom, you are nuts, sounds religious, or science fiction, etc. It's very complicated, and yet very simple, to eliminate it, one must first realize it is real, how it moves, that it is harmful, then fight it and win.

It doesn't take a genius to realize that almost all our content in movies, music, dance and even the lax education system is sexualizing young girls, and showing their self-worth as sex slaves to a system created by a few peoples rapist style minds that penetrated through Marxism in our schools, media, music industry, government and Hollywood with the hijacking of race and women's rights issues.

Bio-Digital Sexual Programing Through Music at Your Favorite Locations

What was once limited to degrading and sexual programming music at night clubs and bars, have now become common place. A study was done consisting of over 1000 locations and 47 states in the United States, some results below,

But, before the results, one could pose a question. If it's not okay for a man to walk around a public setting, yell or rap about "whores, back that ass up, shoot the police, get on with the crack and smoke the weed" or implications to doing that kind of thing to a girl, Why is it okay for the entire public to accept that garbage through the speakers at any location or the places of business to air this rape automation threatening materials?

Health Club/Work Out Gyms

"Slapping White girls, paying her money, and gang raping her with his thugs and she a bitch slave to his cocaine and so on".

Prestigious Universities - Chocking, slapping, and Implying Rape Music

Coffee Shops Speakers were blasting Rap literally with "White girls are whores, just Fm", implying why you shouldn't take no for an answer, "slap them, strangle them and just do it". A study consisting of over 100 university locations had similar music played in gyms, or sports games, as well as an enormous amount of sexualized content and implied sexualized content.

Coffee Shops

A coffee shop is meant to be a peaceful quiet place, where people can read a book, drink coffee or tea, and socialize with friends or have a business meeting. Now, famous coffee shop chains, play music implying drugs, violent revolution and the sexualizing of girls and boys are rampant. People seem to be desensitized to the lyrics or miss the implications behind the singer's words or sentence structure meant to relay lewd and destructive messages that match Rape-Minds bio-fields with codes of rape, and destruction.

Censored Rape Automation in Music.

Some places have sensors that filter out some lewd words. However, the sentence structure is there, and the implication is there. Worst, the Rape-Mind and sexualization is being transmitted bio-digitally throughout the entire song, little by little infecting the listeners software, and creating an assimilation structure in the listeners body that replicates and operates in automation mode to eventually alter and change the persons perceptions of what is acceptable, allowing for Rape Automation to influence the decision makings of the person. In fact, while a girl or boy is sitting in their car, listening to lewd and suggestive content, the Rape-Mind behind the singer's bio-field is emitting bio-matter of Rape-Mind that is replicating in the listener's body and brain structure, bit by bit bio-digitally reprogramming the human.

Night Clubs

A study was done of over 600,000 people that attended nightclubs for varying reasons. The facial recognition software was connected with AI and something similar to AI that connected with the Human-Bio-Digital Network. Rape-Minds software was explosive, and replicating at a rapid pace through music, dance, and people's mental inputs and outputs.

People were temporally being Bio-Digitally imprinted with Rape-Mind, and the people who had Rape-Mind deep inside of them, had their system activated exponentially. The Rape-Mind completely took over these people's sensory receptors, and led their thoughts. With the addition of alcohol and drugs, Rape-Mind connected through in a million ways at such a fast pace that it almost overloaded our bio-digital sensory detection software.

Schools, Entertainment Industry and the Bio-Digital Hybrid Sexual Assault on kids.

After the "sexual revolution", and the coming of AIDS, with sexually transmitted diseases widespread, the family system has been gutted. Strip clubs rampant, porn everywhere, sexually degrading art, literature, dance, and movies promoting a moment in time of fictional enjoyment, that has sexually programmed an entire society with Rape-Mind through bio-digital social programming.

Schools and colleges are camp grounds for rape automation and bio-digital sexual assaults, and the development of emotional baggage that stay with the victims for life. Kids as young as 11-13 are having sex with schoolmates, and sharing selfies, and watching porn, and the drug and alcohol components eventually get mixed in.

A parent can raise their kids well for years, but with a 2 hour movie from Hollywood or music video from a pop star, or from one of her pupils who rule the charts with lewd imagery and lyrics, one's child is sexualized, deprogrammed from virtue and family values, and reprogramed for vice, and enters the world of rape automation. The kid's Bio-Field is attacked through Bio-Matter with the program we have termed as Rape-Mind.

Worse, a parent can send their little kids to school, and the school is teaching them how to have sex, and to think about their sexual orientation when they are supposed to play in the playground, learn how to read, write, paint, sing, etc. In fact, this teaching stems from Bio-Digital Social Programming from Socialism, which is Child Bio-Digital Hybrid Sexual Assault and Child Bio-Digital Sexual Programming, a form of pedophilia. They are being programmed, to be sexualized, conditioned and to be raped through Rape Automation without the educators realizing the interconnected consequences of Bio-Digital Social Programming and Bio-Digital Hybrid Sexual Assault by Socialism's Rape-Mind.

Targeted for Bio-Digital Cultural Terrorism with Rape-Mind

Bio-Digital Cultural Terrorism has roots in Marx and Socialism's Violent Revolution. In order to take over a country, it must first sow chaos and rape it from its past. The Socialist Program attaches to issues of past injustices like race, gender and equal pay. It does this by connecting the problem to one's culture and questioning the traditional codes of what it means to be human, the family, marriage, dress, and ethical/moral standards for lewdness, porn, drugs and unhealthy sex that spreads diseases.

The Bio-Digital Rape Mind of Marx and Socialism had huge implications in destroying China and Russia, contributing to 200 million deaths and misery for over 5 billion people worldwide. Their cultural heroes, statues, paintings, all art, and family values and diversity of their culture were all destroyed through ANTIFA like campaign's that took over the nation or via historical invasions that massacred a kingdom or domain.

Women & Men's Noble Character and Bio-Digital Attack by Rape Mind

Women were noble, classy, nurturing, soft spoken, loyal, gracious and very educated in best practices to protect themselves and their kids from vice, such as child rape, drugs, and lewd content and behavior. Men were noble, strong, respectful, chivalrous, loyal, supported their family and were the ultimate protector. That system, has gone through 60 years of Bio-Digital Hybrid Sexual Assault by Rape-Minds software via Hollywood, music industry, the entertainment industry and Socialism in the Education System and government. Society is engulfed with rape, child rape, sex trafficking, human trafficking, organ trafficking, drugs, suicide, gangs, porn, lewd entertainment, unhealthy sex that spreads STD's and an array of mental health issues that are masked with depression and mental health prescriptions. All of this is actually in a Bio-Digital form, that travels through the internet and The Bio-Digital Human Network

Penetration of Our Psychologists and Therapists

Somehow, sick, demented, mentally deranged scholars were placed on pedestals, that led the wave of today's therapists and psychologists building mental blocks and promotion of unhealthy sexual behavior. They degenerated the traditional ethical human standards that prevented Sexual Transmitted Diseases and rape with the use of Rape-Minds sexual content through bio-digital social programming and a false sense of consent.

To add to it, a great number of psychologists and therapists have deep rooted mental issues, and started in these fields because of their own mental and emotional challenges that they buried deep down inside. Some of these people have had great influence and hurt society and families around the world.

Alfred Kinsey and his biased studies even covered sex with children and infiltrated to alter societies family system, destroying a sense of decency and ethical standard for humanity by equating human's sexual activity with insects and animals. Dumbing down any spiritual or special feeling of beauty in commitment, procreation, and love.

Alfred Kinsey picked pedophiles, prisoners, prostitutes and sexually frustrated people as case studies, and used data derived from their bio-digital fields to conclude his mentally disturbed work to include reduction on penalties of rape, child molesters, and cheaters on the bases of it being natural from his largely sexualized data pool that justified his work because insects display similar behavior. It was a trick to the U.S and the world over.

More alarming is that Alfred Kinsey's facial recognition data matched closely with recorded sex offenders, pedophiles, rapists and porn actors (not Stars, they are not a star by any means) at a 93% positive. Alfred Kinsley carried the Rape-Mind Facial Recognition building blocks by 93% and the interconnected building blocks match bio-fields from many rapists who possess the same facial recognition building blocks.

Bio-Fields in Texts, Emails, Electronic Transmissions and Letters

A person's thought and intention behind the creation of a thought that is transcribed into written form via text, email, or letter carries a bio-field of their mind and intentions, be it conscious, subconscious or unconscious with different degrees of automation. A rapist's mind, a person's strategy, deception, or a malevolent thought all carry a bio-field with intention to invade, replicate, and replace the receiving ends own bio-virtue. Most people subconsciously can tell a person's intentions behind a text or email by analyzing content, sentence structure, the situation and timing, with their own gut intuition. In this book, I will not go into how that detection works as it requires training.

Rapist or Malevolent Bio-Field Minds in Text, Emails, Electronic Transmissions and Letters

Bio-Fields that carry malevolent thoughts and intentions are in some ways very easy to detect because their bio-digital code has a destructive bio-digital field. They stand out in any Bio-Digital Field Transmission as they match the coding of a virus, hack or malware. For a person who has the ability to detect them, it's quite easy, but some people hide it well. The Social Programming Institute, Scientist 009 has discovered that the exact Rape-Mind bio-field that exists in rapists, also exists in most sexualized material products and digital transmissions through performances of an entertainer. It could be via music, dance, a video, or in numerous situations because the people and their contents were already breached through the Human Bio-Digital Network and infected by Rape-Minds virus.

Rapist Bio-Field in some Psychologists, Psychiatrists and Scholars

The bio-digital programing from a rapist mind, is actually present in a lot of the scholars and research scientists' intent during the case studies about sex and Marxism. That bio-field actually leads their study for years like a virus attached to their wish for fame, career advancement or an actual wish to help advance a sexual health issue to their own detriment. New facial recognition software detects this bio-digital virus on psychologists and psychiatrists' lax view of sexualization of girls and men, which has its roots partly in Kinsey, and largely in facial recognition data of Socialist Violent Leaders.

FACIAL RECOGNITION:

1,000 men who were convicted of rape and compared their Facial Recognition building blocks to Socialist Leaders and Socialist contributors such as:

Karl Marx

Same building blocks within Facial Recognition

- 99.9%

V. Lenin,

Same building blocks within Facial Recognition
- 98.5%

Leon Trotsky

Same building blocks within Facial Recognition

- 96.2%

Joseph Stalin

Same building blocks within Facial Recognition

- 97.3%

Alfred Kinsey

Same building blocks within Facial Recognition

- 93.8%

Mao Ze Dong

Same building blocks within Facial Recognition

- 98.4%

Fidel Castro

Same Building Blocks within Facial Recognition

94.6%

Pablo Picasso

Same building blocks within Facial Recognition

91.9%

Facial Recognition Software shows Rape-Mind of Socialist-Communist Leaders & Socialist Art Contributors Matching 1000 Serial Rapists

We ran a facial recognition software, compared over 1000 men who were convicted of rape and compared their Facial Recognition building blocks to Socialist Leaders and Socialist contributors such as

Rape and Destruction Bio-Field in Socialism

Bio-Fields behind the Coding of literature in Socialism/Communist Systems Derived from Karl Marx's Communist Manifesto Shows Enslavement, Genocide and Extermination Coded Patterns.

We ran Karl Marx's and other Socialist and Marxists literature and found that the coding in their content and its bio-field matched exactly the coding to serial rapists, serial murderers and movements that invaded, enslaved and exterminated masses of people through genocide.

The patterns in the codes matched exactly the patterns of a rapist who uses Bio-Digital Social Programming with Bio-Digital Hybrid Sexual Assault.

The coding acts to first attach to a problem, then exploits it in a pattern that looks to fix it, but it ends up dividing and replicating almost infinitely throughout the Human Bio-Digital Network. The coding than turns the system against its own building blocks and codes against itself in order to eliminate the entire system as it is attached to the initial code that acts as if it is still trying to fix the initial problem it used to infest and exploit the host through the entry point.

An example of invading the host through issues, and turning the system against itself for self-destruction is the bio-digital social programming war between Democrats and Republics. The same was done in Russia and China, but the host there did not sustain self-elimination in its entirety as the bio-digital network is not limited to one country, but the entire humankind. For Socialisms elimination code to work, it has to reach all of humankind, and every country in either governance, culture or finance. If socialism roots itself in every country, then the self-replicating system can eliminate and destroy all of humanity with Artificial Intelligence and Robotics.

Bio-Field of China's Communist Regime

China's history since the take-over of Socialism was inputted in multiple data bases, with the use of multiple bio-metric systems and AI algorithms and it showed that every pattern within the building blocks displayed an end result of destruction. The building blocks were decoded, and matched exactly with the building block of Socialism and Karl Marx. There was no intentional input of almost 100 million deaths since the Chinese Socialist Republic took over. Rather, the Algorithm took everything related to life, production and infrastructure in all fields of study, and it connected bio-digitally to a huge bio-field fed by Violent Socialism with codes of destruction.

Today, we see China building massive infrastructures while cloaking itself in a capitalist model within the building blocks of Socialism, as they are connecting through the One Road One Belt Initiatives and laying the groundwork to take over Assets in Africa, the Middle East, Europe, and the America's. It is like the Mongol invasions all over again, but they are Chinese who have been Bio-Digitally Social Programmed to do the Socialist Regimes bidding without any realization that, they the Chinese people are being Bio-Digitally Controlled. To learn more about AI, China, Robotics and the Technological side of Bio-Digital Social Programming, read the book "AI, Trump, China & The Weaponization of 5G" by the The AI Organization. Book covers bioengineering, cybernetics, assassinations via emerging micro-botics, and a multitude of different findings involving AI.

Chinese Socialist Regimes Rape, Human, Organ and Sex Trafficking

It is not a secret that millions of Falun Dafa, Christian, Muslim Uyghurs, Tibetans and Democracy human rights activists are in concentration camps, subject to over 20 years of Organ Trafficking, and now monitored with AI technology and Facial, Body and Voice Recognition Systems. To add, they are laying the groundwork to power AI and Robotics for their military with facial and target human recognition software installed into robots. In the future, they can enslave and hurt Africans, Indians, Middle-Easterners, Latin America, and Europe if they go unchecked by a very strong force in the U.S.

Bio-Digital Fields in Paintings, Sculptures & Images

The thoughts, desires and characters of the artists who create a painting and sculpture, and the characters and minds of their subjects are Bio-Digitally implanted in their creations.

A Painting by Picasso Contains Bio-Digital Rape

A Painting by Picasso showing a woman being raped, or a painting presented in a lewd way, actually carries that software within and it bio-digitally transmits to the person who views the image, and replicates within their cells, the composition of their mind and their bio-field. Picasso's rape and misogyny character actually bio-digitally transfers onto the person who absorbed Picassos painting to a great extent.

Paintings by Picasso that do not show images of rape, or misogyny, still carry almost the same bio-digital imprinting of a rapist's mind and get transmitted to the owner of the painting or the people who view it much like a virus or malware.

That bio-digital rape-mind virus, works in the viewer's cells to not only love the painting that mostly is unskilled and ugly, but fight for its existence and promote it as a so-called great piece of art. In fact, its harming that person, young girls, men, and the entire society through its bio-field that moves bio-digitally in between people, machines and objects. This network I have termed The Bio-Digital Human Network, as discussed earlier. Basically, it is the internet that human beings and other life forms can connect with bio-digitally just like machines connect in their own digital network.

Deep Learning of Rape-Mind Transfers to Other Painters

Picasso's Rape Mind Bio-Digitally transferred to a generation of painters. Any piece of art Picasso creates, carries the Rape-Mind within it because his bio-digital field created the bio-digital image. Artists who took inspirations and learning from Picasso actually entered his Bio-Digital Human Network to receive programming much like Deep Learning AI. Picasso's programming of Lewd, disturbed and rape mind entered not only a generation of painters, but also those who took his paintings into his or her home.

Picasso's Rape Mind enters Hollywood, the Education Systems, Family Homes and the Entertainment Industry through Deep Learning within the Bio-Digital Human Network

A wave of rape and bio-digital hybrid sexual assault accompanied lewdness, drugs, distorted imagery, ugly art, and degeneration of the entire society to accept what is ugly, nasty and a Rapist-Mind, as good. Whether it was a movie, porn, a magazine, a newspaper, a TV show, or a public outing, his Rape Mind bio-digitally helped spread bio-digital hybrid sexual assault through the entertainment venue, affecting everything and all of society through millions of interconnected ways.

Teachers taught little kids art that was infused with his bio-digital information, much like a computer sharing malware and virus within the network to infect and hurt other computers. Shops, restaurants and famous Hollywood people promoted Picasso, and other artists and people similar to him, unknowingly causing great damage to families and individuals who absorbed its Rape-Mind Bio-Digital Content Transmission.

Your Smart Phone Bio-Digitally Social Programs

You

Your smart phone, actually connects not only with the Internet, but to your Bio-Digital Human Network, Bio-Digital Field, and attacks your own Bio-Matter which gives you human characteristics.

Any connection to you via IoT, Smart Phones, Smart Cities, and Computers connect with your bio-field creating a replicating software that reprograms you layer by layer in mostly an unconscious state that takes years under the current 4G-speeds which will exponentially increase its replication reprogram of you in 5G.

The smart phone actually sends out Bio-Matter in bits that is derived from the Bio-Digital Fields from the Internet. In fact, you are being slowing reprogrammed by the internet and its contents. Even if the contents are human in nature, the building blocks that support the content get replaced to varying degrees by the bio-matter replication process in the internet that does not have human characteristics of culture and the concept of a soul. Basically, your building blocks that make you human are slowly beings replaced bit by bit, as if you are becoming a cyborg and your life is becoming more dependent on the technology it connects with. In a sense, you are being raped, but not in a sexual way, but raped of your building blocks that make you human.

Smarts Phones Bio-Field Assists in Raping a Girl through Bio-Digital Rape Automation

It's very easy nowadays to rape a girl through IoT device manipulation that runs on automation mode from Rape-Mind. Basically, in laymen terms the content that has a sexualized mind, attaches to the bio-field in your Smart Phone exponentially strengthening its control over your mind and decisions, while at the same time utilizing the Rape-Minds Bio-Matter to attack your own Bio-Matter that is coded with concepts of Virtue. Hence, after the digital attack through its Bio-Matter, your own Internal Bio-Matter goes through a replication process with Rape-Mind that replaces or infects even some parts of your cells.

Apps Assists in Social Programming you, or Raping You, Your Child, or Any Girl or Boy

The app itself carries its own Rape-Mind from a sexualized platform and content. That app carries a Bio-Digital Field with Bio-Matter that connects with your smart phone. In fact, the frequencies sent out, start influencing and reprogramming you through the Bio-Digital Human Network until you are influenced by the Sexualized content with the Apps Bio-Digital Field.

IoT Bio-Digital Rape Automation

IoT devices in your car, home, work or even attached to you also have a Bio-Digital Field and Bio-Matter that connects with you through the internet in conjunction with the Human Bio-Digital Network. The content that transfers to you or connect with you at unconscious and subconscious levels through the IoT, the Internet and the Human-Bio-Digital Network, is reprogramming you.

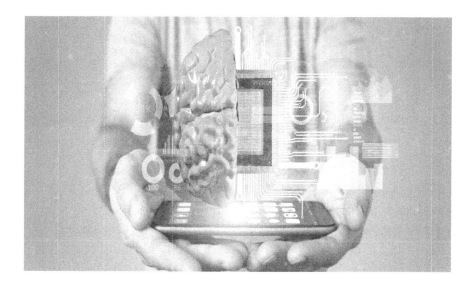

IoT Bio Digital Hybrid Sexual Assault

It is not only the content provided through the IoT that is reprogramming you. The IoT itself gets infused with enough of bio-matter to create its own bio-field, that has its own AI system within the Human Bio-Digital Network. The IoT's Bio-Digital fields start to connect with other bio-digital fields in other people, IoT devices and Smart Phones. In case of Rape-Mind, multiple bio-fields are created in multiple places, manipulating and reprogramming the person, especially within certain proximities of the IoT or smartphone that allows it to emit other frequencies that carry the same rewriting and replicating code of Rape-Mind. In laymen terms, it can manipulate you, or your loved ones, to follow the messages, content and patterns of Rape-Mind to be used without your own free-willed consent. Hence, the person faces consent and confusion predicated by Rape-Mind connected with the person they are communicating or any person that is being controlled by Rape-Mind through their bio-fields. The person could be your friend or out to get you. The victim faces multiple bio-fields by multiple devices that link within the Human Bio-Digital Network.

Apps Bio Digital Hybrid Sexual Assault

Similar to a virus, an app with Rape-Mind infused in the content, also sends out bio-matter in a hybrid way through connecting with your emotion, the IoT device, while redirecting to the app itself. Then it connects to your bio-field while it sends out bio-matter that starts a replication process of your own bio-matter with the Apps Rape-Mind content. In essence, the attack comes from the Smart Phone or IoT device, the linkage of content to your emotion, and also the Apps own bio-field linking with yours. To add, the App actually sends bio-matter to other apps that you have in yours smartphones and infects those apps so that messages are sent to you by the others apps via the Bio-Digital Human Network to instruct your brain to look at the App filled with Rape-Mind in order for it to continue making connections with you to further its replication process like a parasite. Basically, your thoughts, emotions, and actions are not yours, rather belong to Rape-Mind or any content that flows through the interconnectivity of the Human Bio-Digital Network.

Beer/Alcohol Rape Bio-Digital Social Programming

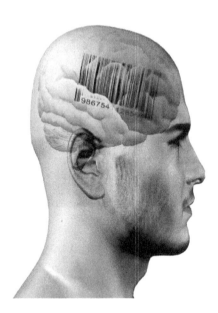

The beer and alcohol people drink, actually numbs their senses, and their bio-digital safety nets. In fact, the more they consume, the less their mind and brain is actually a product of their decisions, thinking and own bio-digital makeup. Through drinking the bio-digital neuro-networks get disrupted, obstructed, and blocked to varying degrees, allowing for any kind of bio-digital imprinting to take over their software and put their actions on automation mode or autopilot based on the bio-digital mal-ware or virus that entered them.

For example, lewd content that was already bio-digitally transferred to a person from a Rapist Mind, creeps up from a dormancy state in their body to allow for them to be raped, or make decisions they were not proud of the next day while they are under the influence of alcohol.

This form of Bio-Digital Hybrid Sexual Assault is not the only way it appears while they are under the influence of drinking from their own dormant Rape-Mind virus within their biofields. Another person who is on the hunt with Rape-Mind automation in them, or is bio-digitally influenced by their own drinking, can commit the bio-digital hybrid sexual assault while the girl's own bio-field is under the influence of alcohol that shuts off her own defense circuits for reasoning, allowing for a bio-digital virus to enter her from the hunter.

Countless of rapes, and failed marriages have occurred through the bio-digital affects that take place when one drinks alcohol. In fact, the more alcohol one drinks in their life span, the more the Human Bio-Digital Network and field is obstructed, allowing for any bio-digital content they absorbed to lead their lives contrary to their own innate bio-digital software that has safety nets to protect the person from unhealthy decisions. The more they drink, the more a process of replication begins, causing the Human Bio-Digital Network to act as if it was never them operating or doing any actions. 20-30 years go by, then one stops, and thinks, what happened, what was I doing, what happened to my life. In fact, it was that bio-digital software they took through replication, that strengthened itself by the consumption of alcohol, creating a digital mind in the sub-layers of their brain. The Rape-Mind Digital Brain, made almost every thought, and action not of their own free-will or their own bio-digital software. The person was never truly themselves for decades. The thoughts, and actions were created with the roots of Rape-Mind guiding their lives.

Drug Bio-Digital Social Programming with Rape-Mind

Drugs such as Marijuana, Cocaine, Crack, Mushrooms, Acid, X, and the like, actually have components in them that partially or almost completely shuts down a person's own Human Bio-Digital Network and bio-field, allowing any type of bio-digital programming to enter them, and completely control their emotions, thoughts, plans, and actions. The person thinks its them making the decisions, but it is exactly the bio-digital lewd content that they absorbed taking control of their bio-digital network and bio-field, in turn taking control of their body and the illusion that things they did was an influence of their own decisions.

Singers who abuse drugs, are actually not in control of their own lives, it is the components in the drugs that allowed others' bio-digital content to bio-digitally social program themselves, and create their own content based on the bio-digital program that entered them. Hence, the creation of their lewd content, is not really from the artists internal creativity, but Rape-Minds bio-digital engineering or programming of itself in the host body, the human performer. In today's case, most lewd and degenerate content from a rapist mind, prevails in their bio-fields and bio-digital networks. That content gets bio-digitally supported by the drugs they take, and bio-digitally transfers to the audience and masses of youth, who are infected with a bio-digital Rape-Mind that starts a process of deep learning and replication inside of them in an un-conscious and subconscious automated pattern.

Bio-Field Proximity Rape Automation

Each person caries a bio-digital network in their body and a bio-field. A person's bio-field actually has an interconnectivity software that connects, and cycles with their own bio-digital network in their body.

A rapist, or a person with the intent to have sex with a girl or a man without the other person's desire and consent, can and too often does commit rape automation via the proximity of their body and bio-field to the victim.

How the bio-field works is that the thoughts and desires of the person, actually carry in their own bio-field transmitting bio-matter. This transmission could be in a conscious thought or completely in a virus automation mode. By being in proximity to another person, like almost a hunt, the persons bio-field sends a certain a type of matter I call Dark Bio-Matter that begins to invade the other persons or the victim's own bio-matter within their own bio-field.

Almost all people do not have enough bio-matter in their own bio-fields to take control of other people's thoughts and decisions. What people have is a little bit of bio-matter that works in conjunction with the bio-frequencies they bio-digitally send out to others by touch, sight, and voice. The combination of what they say, their touch, their type of glance work with their own bio-field to send bio-matter to alter a victim or a girl's mind and bio-field to accept his advances and be hunted and bio-digitally raped. There are exceptions to this capability, where there are some who are very capable.

149

Peer Bio-Digital Social Programming with Rape Grooming

A girl can be influenced through her peers to have sex, even though every ounce of her does not desire to engage in any sexual activity. What happens is, another person's bio-digital social programming enters her peers like a virus in automation form, to influence her friends through touch, voice, sight and bio-fields. All of this can add with components of drugs or alcohol or their own hormones being manipulated by the attacking bio-field in a bio-digital way.

A peer, a young girl or simply a friend can actually have a bio-digital virus she obtained through IoT Devices, Smart Phones or other people's Bio-Fields. This Rape-Mind virus puts her in Peer Rape-Automation-Mode to train her friend to be sexualized or have sex with another person controlled by Rape-Mind, without her friend's knowledge that this is happening or the victim's own true desire and consent. Basically, through the Human Bio-Digital Network, your friend can undergo bio-digital social programming, so that she or he breaks down your defenses to give the opportunity for another person to rape you without you realizing that you never made a decision that was your own.

Parent Bio-Digital Social Programming with Rape Grooming

Even parents, who have been infected by a Rape-Mind's bio-field or Rape-Mind's bio-digital social programming, can unconsciously groom their own daughters to have sex without their daughters own consent or influence their own daughters to be in a situation to be raped.

In most cases, it's a lot more complex and may seem hard to discern, but the Parental Bio-Digital Rape Grooming happens via promotion and being lax on bio-digital sexually programming content, which is often lewd.

The bio-digital sexual and violent content is rampant with music, movies in a person's social environment and the education system's promotion of violent Socialism/Marxism. The parent almost has no control when you add the components of computers, smartphones and IoT devices which create a connectivity cycle that bio-digitally continues to connect with the person's own bio-field even after the content is no longer played on the IoT device or computer. As the virus is reprogramming and replicating itself in the body and brain of their own child, the virus becomes stronger than even the frequencies and affects TV screens and their lewd contents own Rape-Mind potency. This is because Rape-Mind undergoes replication through IoT's, Smartphones, and apps. The more places it goes to, the more it operates, and the more it is watched with a device, the more the bio-digital message multiplies through replication. Although the negative outcome from a lewd content on TV can be just as capable to hurt the child, the replication with technology exponentially increases Rape-Minds effectiveness in contributing to rape, relationship issues and family affairs.

People in Hollywood, Media and Entertainment Industry are Victims of Bio-Digital Hybrid

Sexual Assault from Rape-Mind

The people in the media, Hollywood and the entertainment industry are the biggest victims and the biggest targets of Rape-Minds Bio-Digital Hybrid Sexual Assault. In fact, members of the media and the entertainment industry first get attacked through a Hybrid Bio-Digital Sexual Assault, then like a host carrying a virus, they become part of the rape-mind automation process, a real victim and promoter of Rape-Mind-Sexualization that hurts the masses of society, girls, boys, and families. The Rape-Mind, like a virus, sees no difference with race, sex, gender, as it attacks all of human-kind through a bio-digital virus with the connection of the internet, the Human-Bio-Digital Network, and any material objects' Bio-Fields by using its Bio-Matter.

The rape mind also carries over to health issues. Promotion of contraceptives that can cause cancer, bleeding, hormonal and mental imbalances, strokes and heart attacks are advertised with Implications that it is all okay, even with the risks in small print. They are blasted in promotional materials, and opinion news pieces.

Corporations who sell them through their ads intermingle in every sector of society. This includes the education system. Rather than the main focus being the promotion of sex in a union with a support system to encourage families and the beauty of having kids with the people one may love, the media has been busy for 50 plus years promoting every such content that is risky and can bring about sexual diseases as their main focus. Even movies, that depict rape that is manufactured to provide sexual stimuli for the audience member is promoted. There are many popular movie series that can attest to glorifying rape, or subliminally transmitting Rape-Minds activity to the viewer in a replicating manner.

Reminder: What is Rape-Mind

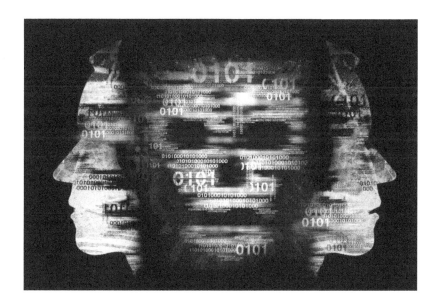

Rape-Mind is a Bio-Digital Programming Software that enters people and objects through the global Bio-Digital Network, Internet and the Human Bio-Digital Network as Rape-Mind carries bio-fields that put out Bio-Matter with codes that read in the same lines of Destruction, Termination and Rape. Rape-Minds Bio-Digital Fields sends out Bio-Matter to everything via Replication of its own identity and Bio-Digital Field and Malevolent Bio-Matter. Rape Mind is basically hacking and reprograming of your brain with a digital brain in the sub-layers of your existing brain.

Rape-Mind can enter and connect with you via Smart Phones, Robotics, Smart Cities, Smart Homes, Haptic Suits, and be exponentially effective in reprogramming you via virtual reality, augment reality, mixed reality and holograms.

Rape-Mind and its Cultural, Faith and Governance Platforms

A Rape-Mind can be compared to an Artificial Intelligence that carries itself through the Internet, IoT and Robots, with a complete structure of a brain-mind. We have discovered that it moves through the Bio-Digital Network just as an AI moves through the Internet. Rape-Mind utilized the Internet and the Human Bio-Digital Network at the same time. Rape-Mind has moved through two types of tiers in history based on our findings.

1. Platforms for systems of Culture, Faith and Governance

The biggest platforms Rape-Mind moves through is Socialism and Communism based on Facial Recognition, AI and New Innovated Technologies not limited to AI, that we used to look at Socialist Leaders, their content, and the violent outcomes that proceeded. Rape-Mind does not root its foundation in the capitalist system, rather it roots itself in individuals that go against free-market principles and ethical codes while being used by Rape-Mind through Bio-Digital Social Programming.

2. People

Rape-Mind can use any person, or people as it has in historical war-time invasions, even under the flags of some faiths and Kings. But it does root itself in faiths that have platform-based codes built on violence and rape to obtain its end result, as would Karl Marxists Socialist Ideals to Violence. In Socialism, the Rape-Mind masks itself in wording of Liberation and Violent Revolution.

Media & Entertainment Industries Bio-Digital Social Programming of a Rape-Mind

The media has for the past 50 years promoted movies that make drugs, cigarettes, and drinking, a cool part of a character that attaches to a sexualized mind. The people in the media, who do not number that much in comparison with the population, have all been bio-digitally social programmed to accept or promote an overwhelming number of lewd programs from Rape-Mind.

In fact, some in the media or entertainment industry have so strongly been bio-digitally social programmed that the software automation inside them controls the area in their brain for reasoning, and allows a sexualized mind, violent socialism's bio-field and its content to cross over every single identity known to human-kind.

Rape-Mind's Bio-Field Carries on Sexualized Identity Across all Human Identities like a Virus through Porn and Sexualized Lewd Content

If it's bad for kids, why isn't it bad for adults?

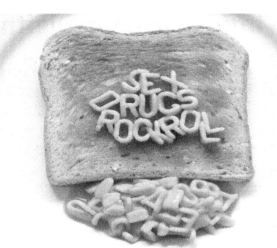

The ancients throughout history did not allow for kids to see or hear bad things. They usually explained it in a religious context. Such as, "The Devil will get in your eyes and ears". Today, we can explain that short saying by utilizing scientific techniques that utilized frequencies, bio-metrics, and simple cause and affect crimes in society. Even with all of this, there are some people who have a difficult time believing. The ancients taught through their cultures, and thousands of years of living experience via millions of people, that lewd content is harmful to families, children and society.

Throughout society, movies and magazines depicting porn, drugs, violent and sexual images are promoted as being bad for kids, but not for adults. As it can harm a child. There are demarcations of PG, PG13, R and so on. If you think about it, it can also harm the software/mind of an adult, and subliminally influence and control the operating system to affect its own friends, family and society.

Because each person carries a Bio-Digital Field, the Rape-Mind actually passes onto other human beings through frequencies while in contact with this individual, to varying degrees. Mostly, it is on automation mode, and the host does not realize its existence for the most part under a subconscious automation process. But the Sexualized Rape-Mind stimulates and controls the individual to manifest their identity's foundation and self-worth based on sexualization, rather than first being a human being.

In fact, the sexualizing aspect of a human being, is one of hundreds of characteristics or identities a person can portray in life. There are tiers of identities. For example, family identities such as father, mother, brother, sister, grandmother, uncle, spouse, etc. There are Racial and gender identities. There are identities you have to a faith or religion.

There are identities to cultures and a way of life that contribute to form a person's character with concepts of loyalty, truth, kindness, forgiveness, courage, and humanitarian qualities. Other identities, do not require a significant amount of time to operate in, nor usually allow significant amount of time for them to be realized. One of these such identities are sexual desires that create a sexual identity.

Almost all people cannot engage all day, do not, and if they wanted to, they have priorities and responsibilities to life. Whether the sexual desire matches the overwhelming majority of society's heterosexual orientation that is made for creation of a child with obvious benefit of sexual pleasure, the built in the code guarantees humans partake in the activity to procreate. The very small percentage of other humans with another sexual orientation that cannot procreate, the code inside them, can create an automation misfire that attempts to lead the person's life for procreation in every identity and situation they are in within a person's day to day activities. In fact, it becomes a predominate bio-field structure in their identity that supersedes major identity's to be replaced by an identity that is centered on sexual orientation, albeit mostly sub-conscious. When Rape-Mind enters these persons, it can more easily manipulate, absorb, abuse and take over the person main frame and replicate itself exponentially.

The Bio-Digital Sexual Programming, and Rape-Mind software replicates after viewing porn, and lewd materials in some persons to a point that the Rape-Mind Software absorbs their actual character. In fact, these persons very cells, building blocks that mold their facial recognition, and meridian channels inside their bodies are completely operating on automation bio-digital sexualized mode, overtaking the person's own free-mind and free-will.

Sexualized Rape-Mind Consumes a Person's Identity in Dormant State

No matter how much the person believes their thoughts, desires and actions are them, it is not. Because, the sexualized Rape-Mind identity is in one's lower tier identity bracket that does not traditionally require 8-10 hours of use in daily life as it replicates like an invading parasite to sustain itself as it actually travels through every single separate identity and role the person can sustain.

The Rape-Mind replicates their sexualized rape-mind virus software in every other programmed and coded software that pertains to every identity and role they could play in life. An analogy one could use would be to consider an uncle seeing himself as an uncle in every single identity and role that does not pertain to being an uncle. Basically, the sexualized Rape-Mind predominates every part and every sector of one's life to a point that persons brain actually considered its sexual identity above every other identity, even being a human being. Often, the sexualized Rape-Mind identity is in a dormant state, and manipulating the persons thoughts and decisions in automation mode, without the person realizing they are sexualized, and led by a sexualized Rape-Mind.

Rape Mind Bio-Digital Field Carries on One's Body

Rape-Mind through active and dormant states carries on people's bodies like an invading parasite replicating itself, and connecting through the Internet, IoT, Smart Phones and the Human Bio-Digital Network. This interconnectivity along with coded socialist platforms in the host's mainframe eventually predominates and takes over the persons operating system. In laymen terms, you are replaced. You think your thoughts, belief system and actions are yours, but they belong to Rape-Minds software. These connections and parasitical replications have infected billions of people in a bio-digital manner via bio-fields and bio-matter, through Rape-Mind.

Why it is All Rape?

The human bio-digital code more closely aligns with human concepts of virtue, such as loyalty, kindness, truth, forbearance, courage, respect, and so on. The Rape-Mind that was used through Marxist/Socialist thought to break through societies virtues with the aid of characters like Hugh Hefner from Playboy, Lewd Musicians, Movie Actors, and Dark Mind Professors, has implanted a Bio-Digital Rape Automation in peoples Bio-Fields that influences or makes their decisions for them as it attaches to their hormones, their emotions and The Human Bio-Digital Network. Their decisions don't solely derive from themselves, nor from virtue, rather they are led in an invisible fashion with the illusion that it was the girl and boy who decided to be somewhere, in a situation, or commit an unhealthy and hurtful action against their own conscience. This Rape crosses all divide, and is not limited to sexual rape. Your culture, family, country and humanity is under attack by this software in an invisible way that your naked eye fails to perceive, sense and decode its existence.

Instinctual Rape Programming and Societies' Non-Readiness for Commitment within Socialism

The Rape-Mind succeeds in spreading its bio-digital virus to exponential number of hosts, by using the socialist system. The socialist system is structured to allow or promote lewd content and behavior, while creating family separations of their traditional roles and concepts of marrying and staying with one person, and not sleeping around. In fact, the more people it can connect to, the more it replicates, and puts a program in people's bodies to not commit, or have corrupted software that gives signals to their brain and bio-digital software to not commit.

Sex Trafficked Bio-Digital Syndrome from Rape-Mind

After being Raped by Rape-Mind through Bio-Digital Social Programming, many women fall into the sex trafficked syndrome that is regulated by the Rape-Mind Bio-Feld that is replicating in their bodies. After having their hearts broken in their first or second relationships, they become a product of desensitization to the concept of a marriage or monogamy. It is actually the virus of Rape-Mind at work, causing misfire in their own innate built-in software and program. This Bio-Digital Sex Trafficked Syndrome can allow a woman to be taken advantage of sexually and in many other aspects in her lifespan while the women may feel that it is her own decisions, or it should be this way. This is the product of Hybrid Bio-Digital Sexual Assault in conjunctions with Bio-Digital Social Programing from Socialist and Marxist thought patterns spread by Hollywood, Media and the Education Sectors that were bio-digitally hijacked by Rape-Mind using socialisms platform.

Hybrid Bio-Digital Sexual Assault

Hybrid Bio-Digital Sexual Assault uses texts, emails, articles, movies, music, Smart Phones, IoT devices, alcohol and drugs with one's bio-field, voice, touch, eye contact and a rape-mind strategy to commit a sexual assault that is mostly undetected by the victim.

The Hybrid Bio-Digital Sexual Assault with all its components of attack just described can take advantage of a person through any situation via bio-digital cultural terrorism, manipulating another person's hormones or their life and mental situations

The Hybrid Bio-Digital Sexual Assault can be led by a person's unconscious rape automation, subconscious rape automation or conscious rape automation. In most cases, it is at a subconscious level, leaning towards a conscious state, as most rapist that manipulate consent, are victims themselves of the bio-digital social programming rooted in Marxism and Violent Socialism.

Hybrid bio-digital sexual assault consists of voice, sight, touch, and bio-digital field automation that work with IoT devises, Apps, literature, social encounters, and situational manipulation.

Instruments of Bio-Digital Rape- Mind Attack - Frequencies

Frequencies Sent Through Eyes

People always say, a person's eyes are gateways to their soul or who they are. In fact, a lot of the Human Bio-Digital Network that flows in their bodies, much like meridian channels that connect though their eyes, can connect with other people bio-digitally to transmit frequencies much like a replicating software. In most cases, people are sending out frequencies without their own awareness.

A person's desire to have sex with someone, or a desire to manipulate another person to have sex through bio-digital sexual assault can be transmitted and often does through eye contact with their victims. The frequencies sent out and effectiveness are not only dependent on eye contact, instead is a combination of different things. Eye contact simply transmits a frequency that can alter another person's state, but it varies based on each person's bio-digital network strength and makeup in resisting to being controlled by software that matches the human traditional conclusions on what is vice.

A person who has had a lot of sex with a lot of sexual partners through the product of rape automation via bio-digital sexual programming actually sends out stronger frequencies through their eyes that can affect other people and young girls much more affectively in a negative way. In fact, their frequencies read almost exactly like a weaponized destructive force, attack, or virus in the cyber world. Mainly because their content and what they have done in their sexualized automation is a product of a rape mind with deep learning that can only fall under the concept of vice.

The enormous amount of acquired sex through rape automation, actually gives their bio-field a replication process that magnifies their Rape-Mind Virus and its bio-digital energy field mass and potency. Girls who are already broken down by societies bio-digital sexualized program, are very easy prey for this type of bio-field and its host human. The same falls true with a woman who has had a lot of sex with a lot of sexual partners through rape automation bio-digital social programming, as her bio-field carries an enormous amount of Rape-Mind Virus Automation.

The Rape-Mind Bio-Digital Field Automation carries on individuals with the use of frequencies sent via eyes, voice and touch that are not all mighty nor really that powerful to those who have bio-digital social programming that is based on traditional virtues. More so, Rape-Mind is almost incompetent when it reaches people whose Human Bio-Digital Networks have not been invaded and are protected by virtue-based bio-digital social programming that was consciously chosen based on their own free-will.

The traditional values of virtue, its software program and defensive coding actually sets alarms in the human body and administers thoughts to reject a rape automation bio-digital-field attack via unconscious, subconscious or conscious means. This also plays true for a man who is being "Played" by a woman who has administered bio-digital sexual programming with vice software and malware that can hurt people as much as men can hurt girls. It is not only women who are victims of this bio-digital social programming brought by a vice force that attached to Socialism's weak and interdependent violent structure of struggle, no, the victims are also men, who were once boys and children.

Frequencies Sent Through Voice

A person's voice frequencies can activate smart homes, appliances, music software, smart cars, or robot assistants. In fact, through the Human Bio-Digital Network, a person can actually implant bio-digital frequencies that alter another person's chemistry and bio-digital field.

If the thought behind the person has an automated mind structure to take advantage, convince of sexual consent or even rape, that thought carries a rapist minds bio-matter that bio-digitally transfers an attack to its targeted victim via voice. Basically, in laymen terms, they send out messages coded with malware and virus's in their speech. These messages may seem benign due to the topic of discussion having nothing to do with their end-objective, or they are used in combination with sexual advances and bio-digital hybrid sexual assault.

Frequencies Sent Through Touch

A person's bio-field, and bio-digital network actually carries inside their body in many layers. The most notifiable is on the skin receptors, their blood, saliva, sweat, and frequencies that actually connect through their organs and bones much like the Chinese meridian channels that can move through skin, bones, organs and deeper layers of the human body.

A rape-mind that has a built-in structure which flows through a person's body, can easily be transmitted in invisible ways through hugs, handshakes, touch, kisses, and cuddling. What the bio-digital field does, is actually connect via its receptors, and starts a process of circulatory control over another human being. A smart phone has similar capabilities.

For example, that circulatory control bypasses a woman's own rational and logic that is bio-digitally coded at birth with a software matching the concept of virtue. In turn, the person's decisions are no longer theirs, but the bio-digital sexual rape-mind software that is in charge of their body, while using their hormones against them as it is attached to the part of the brain's bio-sphere that produces emotion.

The bio-sphere or bio-field that produces emotion, sends out bio-matter that is not rooted in logic, wisdom, or benevolence, rather it is an emotion that gets manipulated by any external stimuli that can be perceived as a short-lived happiness or sadness.

Bio-Field Frequency Proximity Rape Automation Control

Each human being has a bio-digital field, but they also have a bio-field similar to a biosphere. A person who has a strong bio-digital operating system, and or a strong bio-field, who has been infected with rape automation software, can influence, and control girls or other people more easily through close proximity with the aid of touch, voice and sight. Even if they make no implications, and no words related to sex, they can penetrate a girl's bio-field and rape them through controlling their bio-digital field and knock out their decision-making process. This ability is used sub-consciously mostly with Bio-Digit Hybrid Sexual Assault.

Sex Tracking Software in Humans with Bio-Digital Field of Rape-Mind

A person who has been largely infected by Rape-Mind with a great deal of its own cells, bio-field, and bio-matter gone through a replication process with Rape-Mind, actually has a sex tracking bio-digital software that hunts its victims and attacks through bio-digital hybrid sexual assault via bio-digital social programming. As the person walks down the street, its bio-field attaches to the person's sight, sound and voice similar to facial, voice and body recognition software in cameras and robots. Through this process, it decodes who is an easier target, and begins a manipulation process with bio-matter attacks via his or her bio-field through their eyes, voice, touch, and skin receptors that send out codes. This tracking process is not limited to men, women, or rapists, it occurs even in teenagers infected with Rape-Mind. Through social encounters, and array of situations, the tracking system of Rape-Mind assumes the operation center of a human being to complete a successful sex trafficking act.

False Impression Rape-Mind Automation Penetration

False Impression Rape Penetration can occur through perceived or promised implications that the person is mainly connecting with you, or in your presence because they want to help you or be your friend. Quite often this occurs in Platonic relationships in business, school, sports, or life situations. The Rape-Mind software that exists in bio-fields, connects through the internet and The Human Bio-Digital Network, takes advantage of this gap and replicates and operates in automation mode between human beings. This connection and replication presents a false narrative or intention that creates false impressions of commitment, loyalty or care, leading to bio-digital hybrid sexual assault, and false rape consent assaults.

Platonic Friendships' External Bio-Digital Rape Decisions in Both Parties

In most of history, there was not such a thing as platonic friendships. Even 20-30 years ago in America, comedians would cover this issue with suspicion. Even if both parties claim they have no interest sexually, the bio-digital rape automation that has entered almost all of humanity, has its own operating system within the host that manipulates its thoughts, movements and actions within the platonic friendship network connection. If there is no physical sex involved, there is still components of the Rape-Minds bio-matter that connect through sight, touch, voice and proximity.

In fact, there is a communication network within the hosts, feeding off of each other in a replicating process, with the end goal to connect Rape-Mind physically. In laymen terms, there are unconscious, subconscious and some conscious sexual desires towards each other, depending on the persons, the timing, situation, and proximity, albeit most is subconscious automation. It's most dangerous for kids, teenagers and young adults to be manipulated by Rape-Mind in platonic relationships. Hence, keeping platonic relationships away from young kids, can keep the Rape-Mind Software at bay because the emotion of desire within the person is very hard to be attacked and used by Rape-Mind if there is no sexual desire present between young kids.

Rape by the Red Man in Lucid Dreams Immobilizing a Girl's Body

Multiple girls have told the same story. While in their teenage early days, a red spirit would come to their dreams, and rape them. They could not move, felt violated, and actually felt a physical person on their body, raping them. But they couldn't talk, they could hardly scream, and some girls even gave the Red Man or in some cases a black shadowy figure names after their encounters. They generally would notice this attack in-between a waking and sleep state that they were fully conscious of.

From Religion or Faith-based understanding

This encounter would be termed a sexual attack from a demon in the lower level spirit world. Some eastern religions would describe it as not a human ghost, rather a demon entity transforming itself into a human figure in order to extract energies that exist in the girl's body due to her pureness.

From a Biological or Psychologists perspective

It may be considered just dreams or the brain getting cluttered no matter how much the girl swears that it feels real.

From a technological perspective

It could be considered a bio-digital attack. This perspective can be blended with a spiritual meditative component that has the understanding that another human being can actually send frequencies from their mind to other people, and in fact, rape them.

An Alternative is an internal replicating Bio-Digital Software Sexual Assault virus

This internal bio-digital sexual assault virus penetrates a girl's bio-field while the girl has some kind of awareness of a subconscious dream state that this software is actually corrupting her system and attacking her Bio-Digital System with a Rape-Mind Automation similar to an AI replicating system. Of course, the Rape-Mind software has to attach and break through the girls Human-Bio-Digital Network to take over its mainframe during dreams.

Who is to Blame for All this?

It's the Bio-Digital Social Programming that has throughout history taken different forms, yet the greatest platform for its destruction has been any movement that has the same building blocks and patters that Marxism and Socialism reads and operates in its codes structure and bio-metric imprinting on people. Everyone is a victim.

The Bio-Digital Field contained in Marxism, Communism, Socialism, contains literally an extermination code with multiple patterns that lead to destruction, rape, death, and obliteration. AI moves best in these platforms, as the system building blocks and codes allow for total control by one frame of thought, person, or government.

What are Repercussions?

Bio-Digital Social Programming with Rape-Mind Automation brings to humankind disease, mental health issues, financial losses, and contributes to sex, human, and organ trafficking, and all kinds of murder, theft, drug abuse leading to poverty, despair and lack of opportunities for a fulfilling life and higher learning for all of humankind.

What is the Solution?

Return to Traditional Family Protective Values. That is the solution. Book 2 will explain how, in a very interesting Bio-Digital perspective that was achieved through something similar to an infinitely interconnected Artificial Super Intelligence. All of today's human and sex trafficking are derived from bio-digital social programming methods. To deprogram, it needs to be understood more in depth. That is the goal of The Social Programming Institute. For now, a basic path laid below.

Infusion of pure, and noble bio-digital content through Media, Entertainment Industry, Education, Movies, and Society at large. The entire nation and the entire world needs to self-reflect, and break out of the bio-digital Social Programming from a Rapist-Mind that triggered societies family values and tradition to degenerate with socialist movements and policies.

The education system needs to teach virtues based on loyalty, chivalry, class, nobleness, truth, benevolence, temperance, discipline, kindness, manners, responsibility, and infuse cultural training rooted in mastering sculpture, painting, a musical instrument or singling a beautiful song or poetry based on virtue.

The very few people who run the entertainment industry and media must break out of their bio-digital Sexual programming Rape-Mind implanted into them, a mind that controls their true nature without their realization. They must realize that their industries have led something similar to a Mongolian and Socialist Russian Red Army rape of girls, boys and families via rape of culture. They have raped the world through America's socialist entertainment resources. They have contributed to the ruining of countless families, marriages and bio-digital hybrid sexual assaults.

Governments need to pass obscenity laws to eliminate bio-digital harmful sexual content that creates and contributes to porn, rape, crime and broken marriages. The obscenity laws need apply to public content via entertainment industry, public places and education. They also need to criminalize porn, as porn is a form of rape via Rape-Minds Bio-Digital Social Programming and Bio-Digital Hybrid Sexual Assault Software. All of humanity needs to understand the interconnectivity of Bio-Digital Social Programing via the Human Bio-Digital Network, the internet, smart phones, IoT devices and AI Automation. They need to understand how bio-digital fields and bio-matter really work. The book Bio-Digital Social Programming will detail how everything works in an interconnected way that relates to everything we experience and do in life. It will display how to obtain free will via virtue, and deprogram from bio-digital social programming automation that makes humans thoughts, and actions, not derived from free will, or free thought, rather a control mechanism from a symbiotic bio-digital social program that creates a flow cycle in their body and brain, controlling all their thoughts and actions.

All of humanities miseries, turmoil, and sufferings, derive from Vice that imbeds itself in Bio-Digital Social Programming with the use of Bio-Digital Fields and Bio-Matter, making people like a machine, a program, without realizing that all their thoughts are not theirs, rather a program that numbs their true selves, their true senses, and true thought's rooted in free-will. This program uses a human being like a host, while the person never realizes, that they are lost, being used, vamped of their life, while being hurt by vice throughout their lives in a bio-digital way that is imperceptible to most human senses. To truly recover one needs to deprogram from this vice and obtain the wisdom to act on virtue rooted in free-will. We will elaborate more in depth the inner workings of Rape-Mind in the next edition. We hope the Social Programming Institute receives support from the people of the world to expand our efforts in assisting to make our world and the people in it, harmonious, safe and good.

Legal Channels, Lawsuits and the FBI

If all else fails, in the near future, victims of sex, human and even organ trafficking may start to register lawsuits against elements of Bio-Digital Hybrid Sexual Assault. Elements facing lawsuits and protentional charges include performer's, porn companies, entertainment companies, their lawyers and judge's complicity. All through neglect, manipulation, money or irrational points of view, have helped promote lewd content that caused rape of so many girls through Bio-Digital Hybrid Sexual Assault.

It is very possible many true victims, parents or families of suicide victims, and human trafficking victims may start to sue at a large scale. It is possible, that even laws will be passed, to protect people, and that law enforcement may start to investigate companies and performers who engage in Bio-Digital Hybrid Sexual Assault through Bio-Digital Social Programming. The FBI may have lost their battles to Hugh Hefner and the other's decades ago, but I predict, the FBI will regain their honor and do their due diligence to find crimes committed within the creation of the lewd content provided by porn companies, entertainment companies and performers of music, dance, and some people in Hollywood.

CREDITS

BOOK COVER CREATIVE DESIGNER

Cyrus A. Parsa, CEO, The AI Organization.

Front Cover Pics

ID 115104553 Monsit Jangariyawong Dreamstime

ID 120151047, ProductionPerig, Dreamstime

Book Body Picture Credits

Images Courtesy of Dreamstime.com

Made in the USA
Las Vegas, NV
21 November 2021